I Ain't Scared of You

Bernie Mac on How Life Is

I Ain't Scared of You

Bernie Mac with Darrell Dawsey

POCKET BOOKS

New York London Toronto Sydney Singapore

All photos courtesy of the author's collection unless otherwise noted.

An *Original* Publication of MTV Books/Pocket Books

 POCKET BOOKS, a division of Simon & Schuster, Inc.
1230 Avenue of the Americas, New York, NY 10020

ISBN: 0-7434-2821-8

First MTV Books/Pocket Books hardcover printing October 2001

10   9   8   7   6   5   4   3   2   1

Acknowledgments

Thanks to my wife, Rhonda, and my loving daughter, Je'Niece, who have been my motivation. They are my two best friends in all my life. To my entire family, in-laws, acquaintances past and present, associates, and friends. To my enemies, thank you for your motivation! To "Big Fella" and "AV," thanks for thirty years of straight-up friendship.

Thanks to Richard Abate at ICM; Armstrong and Hirsch; Simon & Schuster, MTV, and Pocket Books; UTA. To my editor, Tracy Sherrod—great work! Thanks for getting it right, baby girl! To Darrell Dawsey, for taking my words out of context!

Thanks to my main man and manager, Steven Greener, who has done a great job with my career—knowing me, knowing my style, and knowing when to stay the hell out of my business!

To Chuck, my tour manager, who has been "busted" on numerous occasions. To my hair designer, Teressa, who don't appreciate shit! Just kidding (on the real).

To Haj, my clothes designer, who's been with me an eternity and who's one selfish sumbitch; to my main man, the Big Fella, thank you for loving Bernard, not Bernie Mac; and to my booking agent, Jody Wenig, who really knows how to book me "right" and cares about me. Thanks to my good friend and assistant—they come no better than Geri Bleavings. And last but not least, to my fans, who truly made me and not Hollywood. Thank you with all my heart.

From the Mac Man,
Bernie Mac

Darrell Dawsey would like to acknowledge: God; moms and family; my sweetie, Chastity Pratt, and our newborn son, Khalil Aziz; Cara; Jamil; Natasha; my editor, Tracy Sherrod; Richard Abate; my Manifest dogs; my cousins in Philly; Tom, Kel, Al and the whole team, from Detroit to LA to NY.

Contents

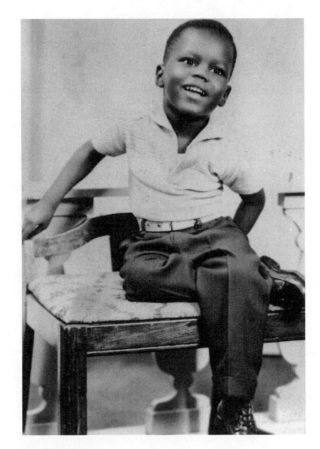

Bernie Mac, age five.

Introduction

People are always coming up to me, asking me how I got into comedy, what made me want to do this. They think it's something a muh'-fucka just picked up along the way to try and make some money. Unh-unh. Naw. This is something I was born to do, baby. I been doing shows since I was a kid. It didn't matter where—backyards, apartment hallways, the alley. I been entertaining since I was little.

I'mma tell ya a true story. It started when I was about four. I was at home with my mama, and I noticed that she had started crying. I went, sat on her lap. And you know, as a little boy, when you see you mama crying, you automatically start crying.

I took my mother's hand, and I was wiping her face. I asked why she was crying. And my mom told me, "Nothing, son. Nothing." The same instant she told me "nothing," Ed Sullivan came on. And he said that he had a "really big shew." And then he introduced Bill Cosby.

At that particular time, there wasn't nothing but four people on TV—four blacks—that was Diahann Carol, Sidney Poitier, Sammy

Davis Jr. and Bill Cosby. When I saw Bill Cosby, he came on and my mother was looking at him. I'll never forget: He was doing this bit about sex in the bathroom. And while he was doing his act, I noticed that mother was still crying—but she had also started to laugh. Pretty soon, she was laughing so hard you wouldn't even have known she had just been crying. And when I saw her laughing, I started laughing. I saw the joy in my mother's smile. When I looked on television, I saw this man making her laugh—even with all the problems and struggles she was going through at the time.

I saw the power of comedy.

Right then and there, I turned to her and said, "Mama, that's what I'm going to be. I'm going to be a comedian—so I don't ever have to see you cry no more."

That's a true story, man. That's what made me want to do this, even after my mother passed. That's what inspires my humor: I don't want nobody to cry.

—*Bernie Mac, April 3, 2001*

I Ain't Scared of You

Chapter One

Hard Times and
Humble Beginnings

I grew up in the streets of 69th and Morgan, the south side of Chicago. Rough as hell. We did all that bullshit—fighting, cuttin' each other with glass, shootin'. But back when we were coming up, we could joke with each other hard. We killed each other with jokes, all day long. And we didn't run and get no pistols or nothin'. Learning how to take a joke, learning how to tell one on somebody—that shit made you stronger. People talkin' about you: "Ya hair nappy"; "You got on floods up to here."

Lint in ya hair? Shit, you had the teddis.

And it's *always* a guy that smells like piss.

"Black ass tar baby," they used to call me. "Spooky Juice." I'm sitting up there, they laughing at me and shit. I went home mad, can't sleep. Next day, I come back: "Motherfucker," I was talking that shit, too. "Yeah, look at you . . ." You learn how to fight back, man. I didn't go get no pistol. That's when I learned to come back. "Look at you!"

Growing up, I laughed at stuff that people couldn't understand. I'd be laughing at the craziest thing, and people would be lookin' at me like, *What the hell? Something wrong with that muthafucka.*

I laughed at people's misfortune—because I had so many misfortunes. But I didn't look at them as misfortunes. I learned hard lessons in life; I had to because I had so much happen: My mother died my sophomore year in high school. The next year, same day, my brother dropped dead. Two years after that, I got married because my girlfriend got pregnant. The year after my wedding, my father—who I had only recently met—died.

That was just life to me. So my mentality was, your misfortune wasn't all that bad because that's the way I thought about mine. But on the flip side, you were like, "This muthafucka laughing. I'm sitting up here, house burnin' down, and this muthafucka up here *laughing.*"

That's true. One time, there was this fire on our block, and everybody had come running out this house. They was in they draws, hair all messed up, and there go Ms. Lee screamin', "Aw Lord, our prop'ty, our prop'ty!"

And I'm laughing. Ms. Lee snapped on me: "It ain't funny! It ain't funny!" The more she screamed, the harder I laughed. But I wasn't laughing at the fire. I wasn't laughing at the fact that their house was burning down. I was laughing at their expressions.

I just kept seeing her face, all frowned up, eyes bugged out, raggedy-ass headrag on, and she just screamin'. One side of her panties was in the crack of her ass. Her old man—he had lost a leg to diabetes—and this peg-leg muh'fucka was just kickin' at the air. Just kickin'. Talkin' to firemen, talkin' 'bout, "Hurry up!"

I just couldn't hold it. I was falling out.

But like I said, I could laugh at people's misfortunes because I had so many of my own. Like a lot of black people, I grew up straight po'. Wasn't no question about whether we was po', either. If you really wanted to know, all you had to do was look in our refrigerator.

You go to some people houses and the kids got all kinds of cook-ies and cakes and ice cream and shit. You know, *snacks.*

But not us. We ain't never have no good food, man, nothin' for kids to just munch on. Shit, fuck around and ask my granddaddy 'bout some damn snacks.

> **KIDS:** Daddy, can we have a snack?
> **GRANDDADDY:** Mm-hmm, yeah, you can have a snack.
> Put you a coupla boiled eggs up in that pot in there.

Seriously, that was a snack at our house. We'd put about three or four eggs in a pot, boil 'em, then my granddaddy would cut 'em up in halves. I'd get a half. My brother would get a half, and so on. Then you'd add salt and pepper *and hot sauce.*

Maaaaan, you'd be farting all damn night.

Everybody would be in the bed trying to get some rest, my grandmama and granddaddy in the next room, and then all of a sudden—*ffffrrrrrppppppppp.*

"Man, why you—why you—why you do it by my *face? Ma-maaaaaa!* He fartin' in people's face!"

"Well, he just did in mine! He did it in mine!"

That's from eating all them eggs.

And it wasn't just snacks. You *know* you poor when you eatin' breakfast food late. You fryin' toast? At nine o'clock at night? With bacon?

You're broke.

We'd have to get some baloney and fry it until the black forms a circle around the edges. Don't even have no bread. Just roll it up like a hot dog and eat it.

And don't let us really get some ice cream. *Booooyyy.* When we'd get ice cream, my granddaddy would give us all one scoop each. I'd get mine, stir it up, mash it, make it seem like I had a lot. And you know kids: always examining what the other kids got.

My brother would be lookin' at mine, and then he'd start complaining to my grandfather—which was the *wrong* thing to do.

"Granddaddy, he got mo' than me!"

My granddaddy'd tell him: "Ain't nobody got mo'! Ain't nobody got mo'!"

"Yes, he do! Everybody got mo!"

Then my granddaddy would just get mad at all of us. He couldn't just get mad at one of us. He had to get us all.

"Ain't nobody got—You know what? Go to bed! All y 'all, go to bed!"

It'd be two o'clock in the afternoon. "Go to bed!"

We all laying up in the bed, the lights out. We just layin' there, eyes wide open, mad. That was motherfuckin' torture. We all in the bed, can't go to sleep. My granddaddy would peek in the room and be like, "Close ya eyes! Close ya eyes!"

Two o'clock in the goddamned afternoon! You hear all the other kids playing outside and shit: "One potato, two potato, three potato, fo' . . ." We can't even look out the window. We just laying in the bed, 'cause my brother done said I had more ice cream. Ain't that some shit?

I used to go to all kinds of lengths to get some snacks. I'll never forget the time my grandmother took me and my sister with her to the market. We walkin' around, and I saw this bag of marshmallows I wanted. And I kept asking her to get us some marshmallows or something. She kept telling me no. So I thought, *Fuck it. I'll get some for my damn self.*

Soon as she walked out of the aisle, I broke open a pack of marshmallows and started diggin' one of them sum'bitches out with my fingers. Man, it was good.

So I'm tryin' to eat that muh'fucka fast—before my grandmother came back and caught me.

Too late.

She came walking 'round that corner, man, I got scared as hell. I started tryin' to chew all fast. Big Mama saw me and was like, "Boy, what you eatin'?"

I was like *"mmnumphin'."* I'm trying to lie, but my black ass got white powder all around my lips.

She walked up on me and was like, "So what's that in yo' mouth?"

I couldn't just start chewing in front of her, so I just started to suck on that motherfuckin' marshmallow, tryin' to get that bitch to dissolve. My cheeks all sunk in and shit. I'm thinkin' if I suck it down, she won't get me.

But you wasn't just puttin' anything over on my grandmother. She was gon' catch my ass. "Spit it out!" she said. I'm still bullshittin' like I don't have anything. Sucking, sucking.

Man, don't you know she just started diggin' in my mouth? Right there in the aisle. Pieces of marshmallow all on her fingers and shit. "Gimme that! Give it here, got-dammit!" I'm busted like a muh'fucka.

Boy, she tore my ass up when we got home.

I remember one time, I stole a candy bar. I had wanted me some sweets, so I took it. I had really went in there to steal this rubber ball. Me and my friends had knocked our ball on the roof, so I went in to Stanle's Store to get another one.

By me not knowing how to steal, I told on my damn self. I'm walking all around the store. First of all, I looked like I ain't have no money. Second of all, I ain't have no note. You know, back then, a lil' muh'fucka wanted somethin' from the store, he had to have a note from his mama.

So I'm walkin' around. I see the ball. I put that ball in my draws and tried to leave.

Now, the man who owns the store sees me, right? And he know ain't *no* eight-year-old with a dick like *that*. So either I was stealin' or I had the blue balls.

Anyway, I made it to the door. The man was gon' let me leave with the ball, too. Now, I done made it to the door—but I wanted some sweets. So I turned my black ass aroun' and gon' steal me a Baby Ruth!

I put the Baby Ruth in my shirt, started walking toward the door. So now, it looked like I had titties—huge, deformed cancer breasts—*and* a big-ass dick.

That old man caught me at the door. He said, "What you got?" I said, "I ain't got nothin'." He knew me, so at first he threatened to call my mama. But then he said, "Tell you what. I'm gon' let you have the candy and the ball. But first, you gotta take that ball out of your pants and the candy out your shirt and walk out of here with it in your hand."

I walked out, and at first, didn't understand the message. But when I got older, I understood: He had given me a break, but he didn't want me hiding the truth. Own up to what you do. We all will get breaks, but take advantage of the second chance. That's what I learned—and I never stole again.

Well, not from him anyway.

Yeah, snacks, man. I wanted 'em, but couldn't get 'em. Even when we would go out, we weren't going out for good snacks. Like fast food? We never had no McDonald's. We had White Castle. Two hamburgers and three fries apiece, and two drinks to split between me and my brothers and sisters. You'd take a sip. He'd take a sip. You'd take a sip. He'd take a sip. And we used to fight about who was going to have the last sip. We'd all be looking, watching—making sure nobody else got that last sip.

Then after we did all that fighting, it would always be my grandfather who'd take the last sip. He'd just grab the cup, swirl the ice around in it and say, "Aw, we ain't even gon' worry 'bout it—*Sllllrrrrrrrrppppp*—Ain't no sense in arguin' over it. *Buurrrpp*."

We'd just be sitting there, looking at him like, "This nigga is *cheap!*"

That's why I used to say that when I got grown, we were gon' have snacks and food at our house. 'Cause we ain't never have no snacks. No good food.

Just beans.

Northern beans. Red beans. Lima beans. Pinto beans. That's all we ate. Chicken and noodles. Chicken and fries. On Friday, we'd have fish and spaghetti. Saturday we ate in church, 'cause they sold dinners. Sunday, my mama made a big dinner. Roast. Mashed potatoes. Hot butter rolls. She made a cake. I couldn't wait for Sunday to come. Every Sunday, we had a good dinner.

Monday? Beans and rice.

That's why with me, it ain't about money. I'm doing great. I was doing great when I was poor. You couldn't tell me I was poor. I didn't know what poor was. We ate oatmeal and oatmeal alone. We'd eat cereal, and my grandmother would pour milk into my bowl, but you couldn't slurp that muthafucka. When you got through eating your cereal, you had to pour your milk in the next bowl for my brother n'em. And when he got through, he'd pour it in the next bowl. I ain't lying. We ain't think nothing was wrong with that.

We ate party meat—everyday. Party meat. I ate the shit out of party meat. Party meat, vegetables, alphabet soup. That was our lunch. Shit, I used to write sentences in the soup: "Help! Please, help!"

I ain't lying. I was trying to send a message, man.

When you opened our refrigerator, all you saw was light. Lightbulb and butter, that's all you saw. But we was happy as hell because I never had a sense of doubt as a little boy, I never had a sense of worry. I guess that's why right now, I'm not a materialist cat because I never had those things around me. Suits? Cars?

Shit, I didn't have a key to the *house* until I was a senior in high school.

We used to have this station wagon when I was a kid. And when we'd go somewhere, we'd all pop in the station wagon. That was when people could still sit on your lap. Now, you can't sit on no laps—but back then, there'd be eleven of us kids in one goddamn seat. And the windows didn't let down in that muh'-fucka, either. We'd look like the Beverly Hillbillies, everybody's face all smashed up against a window, complaining to my grand-daddy.

"Grandddaddy, his knee in my side!"

"Move ya gotdamn knee! Move ya knee. Move ya knee. Move ya knee. Move ya knee!"

That was the thing about my granddaddy: Whenever he warned ya, he would always tell ya things four, five times.

"I ain't gon' tell ya no more. I ain't gon' tell ya no more. I ain't gon' tell ya no more. I ain't gon' tell ya no more. Let me have to tell ya again."

He ain't *never* say nothing once.

"You kids, don't let me come up there! Let me come up there. Let me come on up there. You want me to come up there? I'll come up there. But you don't believe it, though. You don't believe it. You just don't believe it. Don't believe it. Hmmph, he don't believe it."

We'd be like, *Why does he always have to say the same shit four, five times?*

Like if I was messin' up in school, he'd tell me, "The teacher wants me to come up to your school. If I got to come up to school, I'm gonna bust your ass wide open. Wide open. *W-i-i-i-ide* open. You gon' be wide *open*. Everybody gon' be able to see inside you."

And he'd slap you in a minute, slap the shit outta ya. He just liked hurtin' you.

POW!

Bernie Mac, age five, with cousins Corky and Pat.

"Now, didn't I tell you something? Didn't I tell you? Didn't I tell you? I told you. You heard me tell him?"

Then my grandmother would say to him, "Don't say it again. Don't say it again. Please don't say it again."

"Naw, I ain't gon' say nothing. I ain't gon' say nothing. I ain't gon' say *nothin'*. I ain't saying nothing. Hmmph, see if I say something."

My grandfather used to give us baths. That whole scene was crazy. First, he'd spend 'bout 15 minutes trying to get the hot water to work 'cause our pipes would be frozen.

You'd hear him bangin' on the pipes for a long time. Every now and then, he'd stop to yell to us.

Tink, Tink, Tink.

"Is it on yet?"

"Naw, grandaddy, it's still cold."

Tink, Tink, Tink.

"What about now?"

"Not yet."

"Well, let me try this back end."

Tink, Tink, Tink.

"Yeah, grandaddy, it's getting warm now . . . Yeah, now it's boiling hot."

He'd get that muh'fucka to where it'd be like the damn swamp, steam just coming up off the water.

Then he'd just throw yo' ass in there.

You like, *"Aaagggghhh!"* Skin comin' off yo' ass from the heat and shit, and my granddaddy talkin' 'bout, "Hurry up and get you ass in there before it get cold."

Then he'd wash us. Man, he would scrub us until we niggas was *raw*. You'd be bleedin'. I used to have scabs from where that muh'-fucka used to be scrubbin' on my black ass.

And then, after you took your bath, you didn't just let the water drain. Hell naw, not with all them kids. You got out, and somebody else got they ass in.

You'd be cryin', talkin' 'bout, "The water dirty!"

My grandfather'd be like, "Aw, shut up, boy. A lil' dirt ain't never hurt nobody. Ain't hurt *no*body. Ain't nobody ever got hurt from a lil' dirt."

Man, my grandfather came to school with me one time. I was so embarrassed I didn't know what to do.

And you know kids. They parents come to school lookin' all fucked up, people are like, "Who mama is that? Who daddy is that?"

And you could always tell whose mama it was because whoever her child was, he'd be the only muh'fucka in the class lookin' at his paper and writing, tryin' to pretend like he was doing some work.

So my grandfather comes up to the school to talk to my teacher. "Uh, I'm Mr. Mac. I'm here for Bernard Mac."

Then he'd try to use big words while he was talking to the teacher. "So, uh, what seems to be the *calculation?*"

Everybody was looking around like, *What?* Then the teacher told him, "Well, Bernard's being a disruption in class. He laughs a lot."

"He laughs a lot? I done told him about laughing. Didn't I tell you about laughing? Didn't I tell you about laughing? I done told you about laughing. Keep on laughing. Laugh one mo' time."

Kids all teasing me and everything. I'm just sitting there all humiliated, like, "This *ign'ant* sum'bitch!"

And it wasn't just in my school when he did that. My grandfather always tried to use big words, and was always fuckin' 'em up: "See, boy, you know, when you get the job and it's *inferential,* what happen is, it *rederdefried* itself."

What?

When I got older, I'd challenge him. He'd get tight with me— get really mad—when I asked him about a word. He'd be offended that I questioned him.

"See," he'd say, "first of all, you gotta *abstract* yourself from all the *inferentials.*"

So I'd ask, "What you say?"

He'd get tight. "Don't play with me, boy."

"What you gettin' tight for? I don't know what you talking about."

Then he'd really get tight. "Don't worry 'bout it. Don't worry 'bout it. Just-just don't worry 'bout it. You ain't gotta worry 'bout it. You all *worried* 'bout it."

He'd just get mad at you because *he* was making up words.

* * *

There was plenty of moments like that, too. I'll never forget one time when he was sittin' on the porch with his fan. It was scorching outside this day—I mean, really, really hot. A neighbor pulled up. We all sittin' there. (You couldn't just run around when my grand-daddy was around; we had to sit on the porch.) The neighbor comes by, says to my grandfather, "Hey, Brother Mac."

Granddaddy spoke back, "Hey, man, how's it goin'?"

"It's a steamer today, ain't it?"

"Yeah, man . . . It's about 100 degrees *centipede*."

Ain't nobody even say nothin'. We all just looked around. *Centipede? What the fuck is some centipede?*

My granddaddy was a hard-working man, and wasn't scared of a lot. But one thing he was scared of, boy: my grandmama. Big Mama ran things back then. She wasn't scared to fight him. They'd always be fighting about something. All night long, just fighting. The police used to come to our house so much that when they would just roll *past* the neighborhood, my friends would be lookin' at me.

We'd be at school, hear the siren—*waaaahhhwaaaaaaahhhhh*—then somebody'd say, "Bernie, they gettin' ready to go to yo' house, ain't they?"

The police *stayed* at our house, talking all nice, trying to calm my grandparents down. "Mister, Missus Mac, y'all stop."

Granddaddy'd go on in a corner: "Hmmph. That's *her*. That's *her*. That's *her*. Her be startin' all that. Her be doin' all that."

Grandmama would just be sitting there. "Yeah, I'm gon' show you what *her* be doin'."

"Oh, yeah, we gon' see what's g'wains on." That's where I got that from—"g'wains on"—from my grandmama. Then she'd be like, "Tell ya what: it's gon' be a new day in the week when I get up on ya. 'Cause on the eighth day, I ain't gon' get off ya."

Then she'd get tight-lipped on ya—and she'd always close her eyes when she was threatening him. That meant she serious. Her eyes would close real slow and tight, and she'd always have to add: "I'mma cut yo' ass in two."

I asked her once why she always closed her eyes when she said stuff like that.

"Baby, so I can say it with conviction," she said.

Scared the shit outta me.

But most of us came from that. That's what was real. That was how our families were back then. But that's also when families were strong and were upright. You got pregnant, they sent you down South. They hid you. It was an embarrassment to the family. You were a bastard.

And families took care of each other. When somebody got old or had something bad happen, they didn't go to no doctors. There was always that sick uncle or aunt that you kept in the attic or somewhere.

We had an uncle like that, my grandmother's brother, was crazy as hell. He had had a couple of nervous breakdowns. You never saw him. They kept him in the back.

All you'd hear is him hollerin' *"Hhaaagggggghhhh!"*

You'd be eatin, hear that shit, look around . . .

Big Mama would be like, "Don't worry 'bout what's back there. Eat ya supper."

You'd start eatin' again—and all of a sudden he'd break out again: *"Haagggggghhhh!"*

Big Mama: "Didn't I say eat yo' supper?"

I'm thinkin', *How am I supposed to eat with that crazy muh'fucka back there hollerin' and shit?*

And we couldn't go in the back either. They had a skeleton key where they kept the door locked. That nigga would be back there going crazy. And they'd go and knock on the door and slide him his food. We never could go back there.

One day my grandmother was gone. (And you always knew

when your grandmother was at home because her wig had the little styrofoam stand. If her wig was on that styrofoam she was in the crib; if that wig was gone, that mean she was gone.) So I got my brothers and them and said, "Come on, y'all, I got the skeleton key. Let's see who back there."

So went back there, banged on the door.

He went, *"Haaaaggghhh!"*

I went, *"Haaaaahgggghhh."*

"Haaaaggghh."

"Haaaagghh."

Then I said, "Who back there?"

He ain't say nothin'.

I said, "Why don't you come out?"

"If I could come out, I'da been gone."

I said, "You want me to open the door?"

Then I heard my brothers, "Here come Big Mama, here come Big Mama."

I ran. Put the key back. My grandmother came in, asked us what we wanted for dinner, then went back there where he was.

And don't you know that crazy sum'bitch *told on me?*

He wasn't that damn crazy. He knew my name and everythang.

"Bernie came back here, tried to let me out."

My grandmother ain't say nothin' for a coupla hours. We was sittin' at the table. We all eatin'. Then she started talkin' to me, real calm and quietly.

> GRANDMAMA: So, ummm, you went back in the back, huh? Tried to get your uncle to *escape.*
>
> BERNIE: Who?
>
> GRANDMAMA: I'mma ask ya one mo' time. Did you go back there and try to get him to escape?
>
> BERNIE: Naw, I heard him—I heard him—I—I heard sumthin' fall and I went back there and I asked him if

he was all right. That's all I asked him. That's all I asked
him. I asked him if . . .

GRANDMAMA: He say you tried to let him out.

BERNIE: Naw! I—How I'mma let him out? I don't even
know how!

GRANDMAMA: Ya lyin' to me, ain't ya?

BERNIE (head down): *(sniff)* I—I'm lyin'. *(sniff)*

I mean, I knew to tell 'cause she had that *look* on me, right?

Man, she whooped me with an ironing cord. I hollered. I
screamed. I ran all around the house.

But that sum'bitch used to run track. She was dead on my ass.

The next day, she was gone. I went back there again, stood outside that door. *Maaaan,* I cussed his butt *out.*

"Oh, you's a *punk* sum'bitch, you know that? Wit' ya—ya—ya
trick ass!" I'm all up in the keyhole talkin' shit. "I hope ya go crazy.
I hope it ain't no lights on in that muthafucka. I hope ya go blind."

He on the other side of the door, "You, too! You, too!"

"That's why ya locked up in there. . . . *Hhhhhaggghhh!*"

Grown folks stayed on us 'bout everything. Always tellin' don't do
this or that. Let them tell it, everything was gon' "put yo' eye out."

MAMA: Boy, don't be runnin' with them scissors. You gon'
fall down, put yo' eye out!

Put yo' eye out? How come it was always yo' eye? How come
you never heard, "You gon' cut yo' ear off?" Or "Boy, you gon' lose
yo' nose?"

Nope. It was, "Carry the knife by the handle. And walk wit' it!
Walk, before you mess around and put yo' eye out!"

But what happened to those kind of injuries you had when you was a kid? Lil' kids don't have those kind of injuries now. They don't fall down the stairs. We used to get cut up, bruised, scarred. One time, we had a board holding up our window and I knocked it away, and the window smashed my hand. My nail was all black, hurtin' like a muh'fucka.

Those were the old injuries. Kids don't have those no more. Now, they just continuously get shot. They can't just hurt themself no more.

> BYSTANDER: Man, you heard what happened to that nigga Pierre?
> BYSTANDER 2: Naw, what happened?
> BYSTANDER 1: Got to arguin' with a nigga, and he got shot.

Bernie rehearses for Midnight Mac *on HBO.*

BYSTANDER 2: Whaaat? Damn, dog, how old was he?
BYSTANDER 1: Eight months.

What happened to the kid shit? Worst happened to us was, we'd get burnt. "Get the butter!"
Now? "Shot."

I always tell people how I had it hard so they'll understand my hunger, my desire to succeed. That's why I'm not complacent. I'm not settling for less. I ain't never been picked first to do a damn thing. Even when I was a young dude and we played ball—and man, I was an athlete. I played baseball, football, basketball. I boxed for four years. I always had to earn it. Always. When we picked teams before we played ball in the street, folks used to look over me all the time.

CAPTAIN NO. 1: Give me Jacobs.

Look dead at me . . .

CAPTAIN NO. 2: Give me Bob.
CAPTAIN NO. 1: Give me Raymond.

I'm just standing there . . .

CAPTAIN NO. 2: C'mon, Pete.
CAPTAIN NO. 1: Gimme Michael.

I'm the last one.

CAPTAIN 2 (rolling his eyes): *(sigh) C'mon, nigga.*

I got cut from my high-school basketball team four times. We had practice early in the morning, six o'clock. We had two sides in the layup line. I was on one side, did a layup, shot a jumper. The coach looked at me and said, "You can go." Shit, I went . . .

. . . on the *other* side of the layup line. Did the same thing over there, ran a little drill, layed up the ball. The coach tapped me on my shoulder this time: *"You* can go."

I came back the next day.

Got in line. Blended in. Did my lil' shit. The coach lookin' at me—leaning down, squinting. He said, "Didn't I cut you yesterday?"

I'm looking all surprised and shit. I said, "Naw, you ain't cut *me.*"

He stared at me some more, thought about it, then he said, "Go on, man. Get in line."

I got in line, did a little drill. Then the coach nodded and said, "You cut *now.*"

So I went back on the other side. I'm in line and everything. The coach came over to talk to the assistant coach about something. Then he looked at me.

COACH: Come here!

I came over.

COACH: Didn't I cut you yesterday?

ME (*voice high-pitched and cracking*): Naw. I . . . I thought you had tol' me to come over . . . come over here . . . That's why I came on over here.

COACH (*exasperated*): Psshhh . . . maann . . . You gon' sit here and lie?

ME: Unh-unh. I ain't lying. You tol' me to come over here. That's what you tol' me to do.

COACH (Shaking head): Let me see what you got, man. You taking all this doggone effort. Lyin' and shit.

I made the squad.

I had to work harder than everybody. I didn't start. I was sitting on the bench, just sitting. Everytime he'd say a name—"Frank"—I'd scoot down. Just trying to get close so he could see me. I started stickin' my head out real far so he could just get a *look* at me.

But I wouldn't play. I'd go to the locker room, take a shower, guys teasing me: "Ain't no need in you takin' no shower, man. You still fresh." I'm the Minute Man—it'd be a minute left in the game and the coach'd put you in.

And when you get in, you ain't gonna pass that ball either. I ain't passin' *shit*. Everybody on your team out there yelling: "Bernie! Bernie! *Berniiiieeee!*"

Man, shit, I'm out there shaking and baking on myself. I'm puttin' moves on and shit. Ain't nobody even checkin' me but I'm pump-fakin', takin' the ball through my legs, behind my back.

Shit, I had to get *two points*. At least I'd get in the paper.

> ME: When I was about 14, 15, we moved away to a nicer neighborhood. It was almost like the suburbs. I went to CVS High School. I went to high school and started playing ball and liking girls. I started combing my hair. I started getting lines every Saturday. I started creasing my slacks and polishing my shoes. I just went into a hygiene fit. I started getting manicures. Got into smell-goods. I started noticing fashion and shoes. I had to be clever. People were starting to say, "Mac smooth, man."
>
> Now, before that, I was a nasty muh'fucka: Type of nigga who'd turn his draws inside out instead of putting on a new pair. Wear the same socks and shit. Rub my ankle, and dirt used to just roll off that muh'fucka, man.
>
> Butter over there is my brother-in-law. We been knowing each other for years. He knows. We done talked about that shit. Ain't it the truth, Butter?
>
> BUTTER: Oh yeah, I know how it used to be. I was a lil'

chubby muh'fucka growing up. Take a bath? Fuck it. I'd just wash my socks or something in the bathtub, make the water dirty, come out and I'd be dry than a muh'-fucka. My mama'd be screaming: "Get your fat ass in that bathtub, you lil' nasty muh'fucka!"

ME: You know how you was musty and you ain't think it was you? Swear up and down it wasn't you; shit, it'd be *you* like a muh'fucka.

That was back when you'd get up in the morning and just put ya slacks on. Don't brush ya teeth; just get up in the morning and wipe your teeth off. Take your nail and scraped your teeth and wiped that plaque off. I mean, just a nasty muh'fucka.

I remember the first girl I liked. I had had girls I liked before, but they weren't real girlfriends. They were those girls you just fire on, hit in the mouth when you were younger, just to be stupid.

Pow!

That meant you liked her.

She talkin' 'bout, "You play too much!"

The girl I liked was built. She was built like a woman. She had quads, a small waist, her hair tapered and cut fine. She was cinnamon brown, had some fat, red lips. She was one of them fast-ass heifers, too fast for me, but I liked her.

The most we'd ever done was kissed. But one night, we were in her house. I told her I was getting ready to go. She told me her mother was working nights and that I didn't have to go. I put my deep, sexy voice on and said, "Well, I'll stay a lil' bit."

We got on that couch, man, and she moved her panties to the side. This my first real piece, okay?

I said, *"Daaaaaamnnn."* I was rubbing her, and it was like somebody turned the water on my hand. That's how wet it was.

She laid down, man. This is true shit. I took my pants off, man.

. . . and exploded. I mean, soon as my dick went in that muh'-fucka, man, all I remember is, *"Ugggghhhhhhhhh . . . rrrrrrgggggggh-hhh . . . uuugggggggggh."* Man, I shook so hard.

She just looked up at me and said, "No, you didn't."

I couldn't help it. That muh'fuckin' nut was so damn good, I wish I could've *saved* it!

Not long after that, I started going steady with another girl. First time I bust a nut in my slacks was with her. I was going steady with her. Her father was a minister. I grew up in the church, too. I really dug her.

We talked about sex. We'd grind. But her big fear about sex was, she didn't want to have sex and God come down. Her mother and them had instilled that in her head. "If Jesus come while you're having sex, you're going to hell." She really had that concept in her head. That was her belief.

She got to me with that shit. I'd be like, "Yeah, I believe in the Lord, too, and I—I—I don't want to die on a piece of pussy." I didn't want to go to hell smelling like pussy.

So we would just grind. Man, I bust so many nuts in my slacks messing with her that I broke out in a rash. We used to be on the floor before I'd go home, grinding like a muh'fucka. I'd get that nut and it'd be so strong it'd have my motherfuckin' voice changin'. But I dug her.

As I got older, I got into all kinds of things in the streets—but for some reason, I never got caught up with the gangs growing up. Everybody dug me, man. I never had problems.

Well, actually, I had a couple of incidents, but they weren't that big. I once had a situation where they tried to draft me. They just walk up on ya and try to recruit you.

One day, I was in the alley with my friends, playing football. I was quarterbacking. This one play, I told my receivers to go for the

bomb. I said, "Hut one, hut two. Hike." And they took off running—but then those muh'fuckas *kept* runnin'!

I turned around and there was about five members of this gang,
the Seven-Oh Gangsters, standing there surrounding me. They
said, "G-thang" and put their hands across their chests. Then one
of 'em said, "You in a gang, nigga?"

I said, "Naw."

He said, "Well, you is now."

They took me to a basement and jumped on me. That was part
of their recruiting ritual; they beat yo' ass, then you were a part of
the gang.

But I was cool with the leader of this gang, and he knew I ain't
have no business in that bullshit. So the next day, he told me not
to worry, that he wasn't going to let them force me to be in the
gang.

It was a good thing, too, because two days later the Seven-
Oh Gangsters had a falling out with the Mafia Gangsters. They
had been allied, but now they was enemies. You know: Nigga
shit.

Man, they was shooting each other, coming into the build-
ings popping each other. The Mafia Gangsters had a dude
whose name was Sam. Crazy-ass nigga, but he was more cock-
eyed than a muh'fucka. One night, he caught the leader in an
apartment building and was gon' kill him. He had a shotgun
up to the leader at point-blank range. He pointed and fired two
times.

Chk-chk . . . blam! Chk-chk . . . blam!

Ed turned and flinched, but the shells only hit the two sides of
his jacket.

Sam *missed* him! Twice! Cross-eyed sonmofnabitch.

When I was real young, we lived above a church, Burning Bush
Baptist Church. We was also members. It was one of those small

churches. You know the kind: they got three members—and all of 'em are relatives.

Maaaaaan, we was in church *all damn* day, every day. Monday, Tuesday, Wednesday, Thursday, Friday Bible class, rehearsal. Sunday, I used to set up the church. Had to clean the benches, set the hymns out. Run the Baptism pool. Sunday evening we had Bible Training Union. Then there was Young Deacon Night.

And because we lived right above there church, we had to be there. You know how you wanted to miss school, so you played like you was sick the day before or that night? Or you go to bed early so they'll figure you're sick. That next morning you get up and ya mama tell you, "Time to go to school." You tell her "I don't feel good. It's my head, my stomach, something." She tell you to go lay down.

And I used to really act out: I would chew some food or drink some water so—*bllleuuch!*—I could throw it up and make it look like it was vomit.

Couldn't do that on Sundays.

Sunday? "I'm sick! *Bllleuuch!*"

"Just sit your ass in the back. You going to prayer service."

You'd have to sit right in the damn back. You couldn't miss no church. If the kids was upstairs, we used to slide our feet across the floor to keep from lifting them up walking. If they heard you walking, my grandfather would come up from the church: "I'ma whoop your ass."

Preaching, praying, and everything—and he'd come upstairs and beat the fuck outta ya.

That was them: They'd cuss your ass out and then pray.

"Bernie, sit yo' ugly-ass down, ya black bastard!

"But you know, the Lord been good to me . . ."

I talk about 'em, but my family didn't know any better. They used to whoop my ass. I was always put down. I was always told,

Bernie Mac: I Ain't Scared of You.

"You too black." I was always told, "You ugly." I was always told, "Sit your ugly ass down."

But I guess I was too ignorant to listen. I didn't know the validity of what they were saying, I just kept on laughing. "All right, okay." That's how my mind was, I didn't dwell on it.

I'd go sit down and start amusing myself. And that's another way I learned to act and do voices and be creative on my own. I'd play with pencils and shit. I'd have 'em talkin'. I'd have a GI Joe doll, take my sisters' Barbie dolls and make my own stories. So Ken was screwing Barbie, but so was GI Joe and Captain America. Later on, they all pulled a train on her.

That's how I was playin'. Lil' sick muh'fucka, you know.

There was plenty of shit I got into as a kid, but because I was an athlete growing up, the one thing I really didn't get off into was drugs. I tried. But very, very seldom.

I had a bad experience with marijuana, man.

Back when I was in high school, I used to play like I was high all the time. I'd be slurrin' my words and shit: "Ha-ha. Yeah, nig-gaaaa." Cats would say, "Bernie, *fuuuuucked* up, man."

A cat named Joe, he knew I was bullshitting. He trapped me. He came to the lunchroom and said, "Gimme a dollar on a bag." That was when reefer was five bucks and you'd get 15 joints. I would put money in, but I would never show up. So word got around that *Bernie be bullshittin'*.

But this time, they got a dollar from me and came and got me. They took us over to the west wing of the high school.

Man, they had me doing everything: shotgunning me, had me firing up shit. They gave me the joint with instructions.

> JOE: Okay, puff. Now, hold it. Hold it. Hold it. Hold it. Keep holdin' it. Hooooold it. Let it go. Nowtakeanoth-erone!

Whooo! I was so blowed! And my chest, I could hear my heart racing. My heart was pumpin' so hard it was hurting. It felt like something was pulling my esophagus down. My eyes closed.

Then I just took off!

People just started bustin' up laughing. I was running so fast. I jumped on the bus. I sat next to this lady. I was sweating profusely. My heart was going *bump, bump, bump, bump.*

I said, "Lord, please!" I felt like if I closed my eyes I'd die.

The lady said, "You all right, son? Bus driver, slow down. Something is wrong with this man!"

I jumped off the bus and took off running again. I ran from 87th Street to 69th Street in four or five minutes. Cars almost hit me and everything.

I got home, my grandfather asked me what was wrong. I just started trippin'.

Next thing you know, they rushed me to the hospital. Man, my whole nervous system was shot!

They had angel dust in the weed. That was my sophomore year. I was on medication 'til my senior year.

So, ah . . . I'm kind of . . . ah . . . *anti*-drugs.

After that, I was never really no marijuana guy. It took a while for my body to be strong enough to even be around marijuana. I would have flashbacks.

My buddies would do powder. They would always try to get me to do powder. I ain't gon' lie: I did a line or two.

Every time I came around, they wanted to try to get me high. By you not gettin' high, muh'fuckas always want to get you high. Now, if I got high, they'd have been talkin' about, "Put it up! Put it up! Here come *that* muh'fucka!"

But I didn't know what I was supposed to feel when I did it. I'd seen all these cats spending all this money. But the shit was like an inhaler to me. It just opened up my damn sinuses.

My vice used to be cigarettes. I smoked cigarettes for years before I quit about six years ago.

I started off puffin' a little bit in high school. I'd puff just a lil'. Cool Daddy, you know.

I used to like to smoke so that smoke would come out of my mouth when I talked. It would make you look real cool: "Yeah, I tol' that muh'fucka"—you laugh, a whole bunch of smoke comes out—"hahahahaha."

I started off smoking Kools. Then I started smoking Salems. Then I left Salems and went to Newport. Then I went back to Kool Mild. Then I went to Newport Long.

Then I started picking up the habit for real.

When I started going in the clubs, I started smoking after shows. I was going to four clubs a night. I'd wind down, have a beer, and smoke a square.

A pack would last me a week. Me and Big Nigga. He'd have a pack, I might have a pack. I went from ten to a pack a day. Then I went from a pack to a pack-and-a-half.

When I quit, I had been smoking two packs a day.

When I finally quit, I just up and did it. I didn't need anything except myself saying it was time to stop.

It had gotten to the point where, every time I'd breathe, I would whistle.

One night, I'm in the bed with my wife, and I just keep hearing *tweet, tweeeettt.* I'm lookin' around, all out the window and shit. But it was me.

That next day, I couldn't even walk up the stairs. I would cough and nothing would come up. I thought I had a cold. I was takin' short breaths. I asked my wife to take me to the doctor.

My lungs were closed. I wasn't getting air. The doctor sprayed a mist in me and opened my lungs back up. I had bronchitis of the worst kind.

When I walked out that hospital, I had a pack of squares in my pocket. I said, "Mac, you dyin', man. Is this what you want to do?"

I grabbed those cigarettes and threw them as far as I could. And I haven't smoked since.

I was never an alcohol cat either. I sipped some wine; I threw up on myself.

When I first started drinking beer, I was out of high school. I was playing in the summer league after school. A brother said, "Great game" and threw me a beer. Now, they're smoking marijuana, and I'm having flashbacks. I'm trying to be cool.

I had two beers. Between the contact I was gettin' off the reefer and the beer, I was high as a Georgia pine. It was like somebody injected propane in me.

But I think it's good I can't do all that. Plus, that was a motivational thing for me, watching people who did drugs. I keep saying entertainment is a bad business, man. Cats be wanting you to fall. I used to be around a lot of athletes, and I saw how cats were jealous and were constantly giving them shit. You would see how their games would just diminish. That was drugs, man. Even in the comedy clubs. I saw it all in the comedy clubs.

I'll drink some brews, but that's the strongest I do.

Plus, anything stronger than that and I'm givin' you a lap dance.

Chapter Two
How People Are

I love playing black audiences, I really do. They're the people who made me, them 9-to-5 people who work hard and come out to the club to see you perform. But they can be hard on a muh'fucka. I mean, a black audience will tear yo' ass up.

White people, you can struggle sometimes, and they will still respond. You get off stage, they clap real polite and go, "All right."

Blacks? "Aw, Nigga, you ain't funny!"

They will eat you up. They will kick you down. If you ain't strong, they make you feel like dirt. Shit, black people will keep on even after you off the stage. They'll take what you do into your everyday life. If you ain't no decent ball player or you ain't no helluva singer or you a mediocre comedian, when they see you in your real life, they feel like they can disrespect you. If you a ball player and you messed up a game or something, they'll say, "There go that old punk-ass muthafucka! That nigga, he ain't shit!"

They think you ain't no man or something because you blew a layup.

Or you ain't funny, they think they can just come say, "Man, this old unfunny muthafucka!" Now they think they can disrespect me because I ain't get no laughs. That ain't true, but that's how they think.

Muh'fucka singing the national anthem: *"Oh, say can you seeeee . . ."* Muthafucka *can't* sing, right? But black people see that muthafucka in the hall and let you know: *"Sit* your punk ass down, old hoarse-voice muthafucka."

I'm serious. We take the little thangs to bust your balls with. Movies. Art. You don't see no black folks at art galleries. Am I lying? White folks be at art galleries, walking quietly up and down the aisles, minding their business.

> **WHITE ART PATRON** (whispering): Mmmhmm . . . Ahh, wonderful use of blue here. . . . Mmmm. . . . Say, is this frame real oak? Wonderful. *Ahhhhhh.*

But black folks? We don't fuck with no shit like that 'cause we got to bust they balls about something.

> **BLACK ART PATRON:** Got-damn, it's too muh'fuckin' quiet up in here! Damn, they ain't got no music up in this muh'fucka? This ain't nothing but some ol' bull-shit! Plus it smell like wet dog up in this muthafucka. Maan, I'm goin' outside to smoke a cigarette.

We gon' find something wrong. Why are we like that? That question is always asked.

I've been a White Sox fan all my life, mostly because the White Sox ain't never got respect. I always was the cat who never went first, so I always had a love for the underdog, and the White

Sox were always that—even though the Cubs ain't never won shit. Plus, in Chicago, the White Sox are the black team; the Cubs are the white team. And when you go to Wrigley Field, they make sure you know it. White people own that sum'bitch. You start some shit if you want. Your ass will be thrown over the bleachers.

They run shit out there. You go in there talking that Black Power shit if you want to. You'll have *pink* showing on your ass.

We went out there for a playoff game. There was about ten blacks. Those white folks was smoking, drinking, spilling beers. This one brother was trying to get a little upset. We said, "Man, you'd better sit your ass down before you get humiliated out here." They'll throw yo' ass out. Their shirts be off. They be red. Cheeks be flushed.

There are just certain places you don't go talkin' that shit— rodeos, NASCAR, shit like that. Don't go to no rodeos talkin' that nigga shit: "Man, fuck these white people." Lemme tell ya somethin': They'll ride yo' ass like steer up in that muhfucka. Muhfucka talkin' about Brahma Bull?

See, brothers don't know how to go nowhere and shut the fuck up. Brothers think white folks scared of ya. But not all them white boys are scared. Some of them can fight. But they don't fight like we do. See, brothers, we swing from the arms. We can dance around, back up, bob, weave. A black motherfucka can throw a punch and steal a nigga.

But them white boys? Them muhfuckas wrestle. Those muhfuckas get that Bulldog Frog on ya—wrap they legs around your ribs—and you be, *"Ghaaah!"*

You hear a motherfucka holla like that? *"Ghaaaah!"* That white boy got a grip on yo' ass. Those cowboy boots with that knife in the toe? They hit you all in the shin and shit. They wrestle.

Black folks can't wrestle. We ain't never been no scrappers. But when them white boys pick yo' ass up and slam you on that concrete? And put that little chokehold on you? 'Cause you know white boys like to choke you. Aww, white folks'll choke the *shit* out ya.

Now, brothers—brothers stomp you. It'll just be, *Stomp, stomp*—"Mother . . . fucka . . . I . . . will . . . kick . . . yo' . . . ass."

White folks be chokin'. Your motherfuckin' ass'll be there tryin' to scratch their hands and shit.

See, brothers think all white people are scared of them 'cause we talk loud. "YEAH, MOTHERFUCKA, YEAH. RIGHT! RIGHT!"

But you'll get some of those white folks who don't give a fuck 'bout that loud talkin'. Them white motherfuckas with a lot of hair on their backs? You see a white boy with a lot of hair on his back— he ain't no punk. That motherfucka with them two teeth missin' down at the bottom? They been knocked out! That motherfucka can take a *punch!*

Brothers? We ain't gon' fight long. You look at the average black fight. It's 15 seconds. Somebody get stole on, a coupla punches get thrown, somebody's coverin' up—then somebody's breaking it up.

'Cause we gon' have a heart attack.

We drink. We smoke. We eat hamhocks. Hot sauce potato chips and shit. We don't eat no salad. No kinda vegetables. What nigga you know don't eat no chicken?

So you know, black folks, boy, you get in a fight and hit a nigga in the stomach, he gon' throw up all on your back. We ain't in no shape.

Run? *Run?* We ain't doin' no runnin'. Black folks ain't doin' that. When we was younger, yeah. We would run. But older brothers? Shit, I ain't runnin' unless some gangbangers are chasin' me. I ain't runnin'. Shit, your lips be white. *Maaaan,* shit.

Speaking of fights, you know when you done really got fucked up in a humbug? When you gotta make an announcement. You ever notice that? Black folks, when they fight and shit, they got to make an announcement.

Slap!

"Oh! This muthafucka done hit me in the mouth, got-damn!"

Or "Man, this muthafucka done stabbed the fuck outta me! Got-damn, man, this muthafucka done stabbed me, man! Ain't this a bitch!"

We gonna tell you. We gonna make an announcement.

Pow!

"Aw, *hell* naw! This muthafucka done bust my muthafucking head open!"

We gots to announce it. We're funny. It's the truth. We got to tell you what's going on, straight up. If it's a humbug, we make an announcement: "Man, them muthafuckas fighting!" Like we can't *see* that! "Man, he got a gun. He got a gun!"

They gon' tell you. Black folks are journalists when some shit jump off. We're informants.

I talk about black folks, but really, it's okay to have that nigga in you. You can't forget that nigga in you. In life you gon' be tested. You gotta let a muh'fucka know sometimes: "I'm a nigga!" Ain't nothing wrong with bein' a nigga. There's somethin' wrong with being a "nigger"—but not a nigga.

In meetings, I've conducted myself like a gentleman. White folks say something out of pocket, and before you even realize it, you like, "Muh'fucka, who you talkin' to?"

White folks'll say some shit like, "OK, in the intro to the TV show, we want you to come out and dance. Then we want you and your wife to fight, talk about her like Fred Sanford used to talk about Aunt Esther."

Boy, white folks bring the nigga out you! That nigga just'll *slide* out you. You like, "What? Man, I'll kick yo' ass!"

You can have a doctorate. You tryin' to explain something, some white person say some shit: "But, doctor, you have the vertebra—"

You just snap. "You heard what I just said, nigga?" Your whole voice change.

See, that's to bring out the nigga in you. I like a lil' nigga. My grandmother used to say, "Don't bring out the nigga!"

We had a family fight. Our family was all out in the street. We was fightin' the Tarvers. Me and Earl Tarver was scrappin'. Then his auntie held me—and he got a good hook in on me. *Pow!*

My grandmother was standin' there. She say, "Oh, no! Bring out the nigga! You don't hold *my* grandson!"

My grandmother held him, talkin' about, "Go get yo' lick back!"

She held him. I tried to knock his ass out, that *sumnofnabitch!* Had to get my lick back.

Licks was important where I come from. Licks—and "last."

Oh, a muh'fucka got "last"? When you thought the fight was over and he stole yo' ass? Man, one time I was in school and was fightin' this muh'fucka. And just when they were breakin' it up, the nigga tagged me, man. And everybody just yelled, *"Whooooohooooooo!"*

That fired me up. I'm shaking. Guard all up. The teacher told me to go sit on the other side of the class. I'm all mad. I started scooting my chair up to that muh'fucka and was hummin'. You know how you get so mad you start humming?

Mmmm-hmmm, muh'fucka. Mmmmm-hmmm!

I'm getting my lick back. That muh'fucka got last!

Last make you kill a muh'fucka.

> **BYSTANDER:** What happened, Bernie? Why'd you stab him?
>
> **ME:** He got last.

Man, that's some nigga shit right there. What the fuck is some damn last?

A muh'fucka get a lick in and then they *break it up*? You can't even go around nobody. People talkin' about it. I'd be tight. Can't even do no homework. I'm mad.

Like with the fight with me and Earl. Now, my family was peace-

Bernie Mac and fellow Kings of Comedy, Cedric the Entertainer and Steve Harvey.

ful, church-going people. My grandmother and them was like the mayor of our neighborhood. We wasn't known for no humbuggin' mess. That's what shocked everybody, see. We wasn't known for bringin' out the nigga.

But that nigga got last.

I don't care who you are. You black and wanna see a muh'fucka bring out the nigga? Get last.

I don't care if you a preacher. A muh'fucka get last?

PREACHER: Oh, you done mess up now.

ME: Man, I'm always listening to the people around me, always watchin'. 'Cause people are funny, and if you talk to them long enough, they'll tell you some crazy stuff. You find all kinds of shit to take to the stage.

FRIEND: Yeah, like he tells this story about kids being smart. It was about my daughter. What happened was, one time, my wife walked into the room and wanted to watch something on TV. She told my daughter, who was three, she was going to switch channels. Before she could, she had to run into another room. When she came back a few minutes later, she tried to use the remote to change channels, but couldn't. She kept trying for a few seconds, then she finally checked the remote. My daughter done took the goddamn batteries out.

ME: Hmpph. Kids. You gotta watch them lil' sum'bitches, man. They too smart for they own good.

FRIEND: Some mo' true shit: I'm a cop, right? So I'm always telling him about stories from work and shit. I told him about this dope dealer. Me and my partner, we were looking for the dude who killed this motherfucker. We in the funeral home before anything happens, staking out the place to see if we saw anybody suspicious come in. He laying in the front of the church, coffin open. We're looking at the book to see who signed in.

A motherfuckin' pager goes off.

I check my shit, my partner checks his shit. Nothing. *Damn, man, I know I heard a pager.* But ain't nobody in the church. We finish looking . . .

Beep, beep, beep, beep. There that muh'fucka go again, right?

We walk up to the casket and there this motherfucker is laying up there dead than a pager going *off!* I said, "Yeah, that's the devil callin', tellin' him he late."

BUTTER: Another time, we was out doing a ride-along, me and Bernie, out in a police car. We out on the west side. I'm just showing him some of the shit I do, right?

So we see two other police get out and stop this cat, put him on the hood. He kept looking in the car. Then he figured out who it was.

He said, "Damn, they got Bernie Mac?"

Then he said, "Bernie Mac 5–0?"

ME: I heard that shit and that's when I *had* to get out. I let him know: "Hell, naw! I ain't the police and don't y'all *start calling* me no damn five-oh!"

So then I start talkin' to the dude. The brother is about 19. The police done got some weed off of him. I'm like, "Seriously, why you like this, man? Why you out here?"

That motherfucker told me, he said, "Man, you just don't know, Bernie. Man, this *street stress* is a muthafucka."

I said, "What?"

Brother said, "Street stress."

I said, "That ain't like *regular* stress?"

Street stress! Now that's some heavy shit, there. You worried about whether somebody gon' come pop your ass. That's street stress.

He was on the car, and he was serious, man. He looked up, he said—like he had just worked for 24 hours straight—"Street stress a muthafucka!"

He looked like he was getting ready to break down. He needed somebody to talk to. Like he getting ready to get hit tonight. Like he ain't have somebody's *money.*

"Man, this muthafucking street stress a bitch." He act like, "I'm busted tonight. I ain't got dawg's money." He act like he was getting ready to get out the game.

His boys was watching. They knew we had him and were looking to see if that muh'fucka was gon' talk. He was trying to get up out of there!

That nigga looked up like he was gon' cry and was like, "Why don't y'all take me *with* y'all?"

Niggas don't be knowing how to do their shit, man. You need to study them ol' crackhead ass hoes that be selling pussy cheap. They be knowin' how to do wrong.

Ever see those crackhead prostitutes? The ones with the blue lips? They be higher than a motherfucker, still tryin' to shake sexy. Blue lips, eyes be yellow like a motherfucker, talkin' 'bout, "I'll suck ya dick, ten bucks. Pull 'round the back of the police station."

And that's just what you do, too. When ya do wrong, do it in front of the police. That's how ya do wrong.

Ya hidin' from the law? Get you an apartment across the street from the police station. Ain't nobody ever gon' think to look across the street.

When you wanted by the police just walk past 'em. It can be four police right here, talking to each other.

Just walk past.

FUGITIVE: How ya doin', officers?
POLICEMAN: How ya doin'? Anyway, yeah, we gon' catch
that motherfucker.

And you keep on goin'.

ME: I'm always talkin' about how I'm getting too old to
fuck. People ask me, "Well, what about women your
age? Are they tired?"

Lemme tell ya: I think women are in a different
mode physically. I think they get tired of it when they
get a certain age. But when they get it, they are more
in tune to it than we are. Because when they get it,
their body chemistry just goes to the left. They gotta
have it.

A woman can last longer than a man physically and
internally. She can go longer without. Like a woman
might go without sex for six, seven months. But when
that muthafucka do get it? Boy, you'd better be in shape
'cause she might break somethin' off.
FRIEND: I seen a few that had been celibate for like seven,
eight years.
ME: Oh, yeah. They crazy than a motherfucka, too. A nut
will make you go crazy, man, really. If you don't get a
nut, you will cuss a motherfucka out. You see those
evil-ass women on the job and shit? 'Cause they ain't
been bustin' no nut.

And plus, women got tools. It's so unfair. When God
made us, man, He shorted us. I ain't chargin' His work,
but women got toys—dildos, vibrators, all that sort of
shit—to get off. You can't compete with no dildo.

They got this thang called the Beaver, man. It's a dildo with a little bitty tongue that goes over the woman's clit. Make a man jealous.

FRIEND: *Shiiit,* that's my added help.

ME: Uh-unh. A lot of cats are insecure, man. You can't do nothing with that Beaver. That motherfucka will have women throwing up, man.

FRIEND: That's okay. *Sheeeiiit.* Go 'head, babygirl. Do yo' thang.

ME: Man, women get that thang, they be lookin' like they were electrocuted.

FRIEND: I just be like, "Want me to help you?"

ME: You turn that Beaver on they ass, they don't need *you.* The only thing that they need you for is to be next to them, for that warmth.

FRIEND: That muh'fuckin' nut be getting close, they grab your muh'fuckin' head, pull you close. Man!

I'm not a church person really. Don't get me wrong: I grew up in church, and I love the Lord and all. I believe in God with all my heart and soul, and I'm a born witness that there is a God. But now, as an adult, I'm not one to be all up at somebody's church.

I think that church has gotten to the point where it's a scam. It's a business. The Catholics have been doin' it for years. I think that blacks are now getting in tune to it.

Like the churches in LA. They gotta have all the celebrities out. You got Magic there and Stevie Wonder and all them. It ain't nothin' but a conversation piece. It's about popularity, and I ain't never been no popularity buff.

These people get all caught up in the size of the church and the membership and the preacher's name, and everything else but God. They worried more about the building.

Any time you got a church that look like a doggone mall, something is wrong.

People say they go to church to bring themselves peace. Yeah, they go to give them serenity for the wrong they do.

A muh'fucka go to church on Sunday, but step on the their toe on Monday and see what happens. The do wrong on Monday, get high on Tuesday, get drunk on Wednesday, fight on Thursday, commit adultery on Friday, lie on Saturday—and then they wanna pray on Sunday.

Or else a muh'fucka just mess with church when things're going wrong for 'em. It take somethin' tragic for 'em to straighten up.

Ya blood test done came back. You got a doctor's appointment on Tuesday. I call you up like, "Hey, man, what you doin?"

"Aw, I'm just sittin' here readin' mah Bible. Twenty-third Psalm, you know."

Hypocrite ass.

One of the things I hate about how life is now is that you just don't have quality nothin' no more. People just don't make good stuff like they used to.

Milk used to make bones strong. Now, it makes you sick than a muh'fucka. It'll have you shittin'. You gotta take pills to drink some milk now.

Water used to be free. That shit costs you two muh'fuckin' dollars now.

You used to be able to take medicine and get better. Now, the medicine will fuck you up worse than the illness. You ever see those commercials for medicine?

"Take this for your whooping cough. But warning: the side effects will make your nose bleed, could cause high blood pressure, blindness in one eye, stomach aches, and tightness in the wrist." You like, "Fuck it. I'll just deal with the whoopin' cough."

Bernie Mac at eight years old.

'Cause there ain't no quality shit no more.

Why is that, when you're black and successful, everybody feels like they're part of that and you owe them?

Don't be no doctor. People will come ring your doorbell at three o'clock in the morning.

DOCTOR: Who is it?

NEIGHBOR: It's Antoinette. Pookie sick! He red all
      around the throat.

DOCTOR: You should take him to a hospital.

NEIGHBOR: Well, you know, I ain't got no medical insurance. Can you write me a prescription out? C'mon, this is *Pookie!* You know, Pookie used to play with your son for many years. We grew up together. Don't bullshit. This is me!

What the fuck does that mean? Why niggas always try to say that? "This is me, man!"

NEIGHBOR: C'mon now. This is me! Pookie bleedin' out his mouth *and* his ass!

DOCTOR: But I don't know what he has. Plus, I'm a pediatrician, not a general practitioner.

NEIGHBOR: You can give me some antibiotics to clear him up.

DOCTOR: You *need* to take him to a hospital.

That's when the muh'fucka really go off.

NEIGHBOR: Oh, see, you done forgot where you came from! Well, I didn't! I didn't! I remember when your daddy was sucking dick behind the funeral parlor while your mama was in the front selling hot dogs without the bun! I remember when you used to smell like piss!

I remember all that!

I remember when your brother got his head busted out on 63rd with a pair of click-clacks! Who rushed him to the hospital, got him three stitches across this muthafucking eye? Me! Now, my son Pookie, you can't even give him some antibiotics? You'll get yours!

And they always say, "nigga" at the end, like it's punctuation.

NEIGHBOR: That's alright. Your day'll come—nigga!

Boy, motherfuckers are a trip.

Most of people's problems are self-brought-on. People make bad decisions and try to blame other people for their lives.

You ain't gon' get ahead with seven kids. You ain't gon' get ahead, and you're dealing with four, five women. Or if you lyin' and cheatin' and partyin' all night. Somewhere in there, something's going to have to give. A bill ain't gon' get paid or something. And you know what they say about bills: "Once you get behind, that *is* your behind."

But still, people want to do that and then wonder why their life is like it is. And then you gon' go and get mad at the brother who's tryin' to do something with himself, the brother with triple A credit.

You comin' to his house talkin' that bullshit: "Hey, man, uh, let me use your license plate, man." "C'mon, man, why don't you let me borrow your car?"

Ain't that some shit!? You done tore up your shit, now you wanna tear up mine. Talkin' 'bout you'll get my shit fixed. Nigga, you couldn't repair *your* car when the muh'fucka had a flat!

Your life is all fucked up! Your wife left you, and now you fuckin' her sister. Don't think nothin's wrong with that. But you want respect.

You scream, "I'm a man!" But you don't work. Muh'fuckas come in the house, you sittin' around smokin' cigarettes. You live in the basement. You go in your mama's purse, tryin' to get some change. Talkin' about, "You want somethin' from the store, mama?"

You hopin' she gives you a ten-dollar bill so you can keep the change. You come back home, *"Where the change?"* That shit is high than a muh'fucka. Nigga done bought some cigarettes and a quart of beer. Sorry muh'fucka.

Lil' kids in the neighborhood don't respect you. You want the lil' kids to call you "Mister," but they still callin' you June Bug. You mad: "It ain't June Bug! It's Titus!"

I tell kids: you see him standing on the corner talking shit? He gon' be that muh'fucka 20 years from now. On another corner— talking shit. Or at someobdy's fucked-up job—talkin' shit.

The nigga's at the job puttin' down people who work hard: "You know he wannabe supervisor. You know that, right?"

Like something wrong with that!

"Ol' company man ass nigga. Come to work on time. The shit start at seven, he there at quarter to." The hard-workin' guy put in overtime and here you go: "Damn, you tryin' to make all the money, nigga?"

Bernie Mac with Miller Lite Comedy Search winner Damon Wayans and Miller Genuine Draft representatives.

I used to work two shifts, right? Muh'fuckas used to walk by, "Wha, you got stock in the company?"

I respect anybody who works hard for what they get. People who try. You got brothers who don't work for nobody, who have paid their dues and can work at home taking care of kids.

People get mad at shit like that. Some nigga out there mad. He's just come home from work. He done got wrote up on the job. Meanwhile, you up on the balcony sippin' a brew, watchin' your kids and talkin' shit into the mic.

That's the luxury of paying dues. I got my hat off to anybody who sacrificed their lives to better themselves. Michael Jordan was drinking milk. He wasn't drinkin' cognac and smokin' squares. He flyin' and you mad: "Aw, man, fuck all that shit. I coulda made the NBA, but you know. . . ." Nigga, while you hangin' out, Mike is doin' squats.

Look at Tina Turner. She worked for hers. Her body looks good, better than a lot of 19-year-olds. Now, if she takes her teeth out, she'll scare the fuck outta you—but her body looks good. She worked at it.

Niggas don't want to educate themselves, then get mad at you for trying to do better: "Ol' brilliant ass muh'fucka. Fuck you."

I was reading a book one time. A nigga told me, "Man, put that shit down and come on over here and smoke this joint!"

I said, "I'll tell you what you do, muh'fucka. I'll smoke that joint if you read this book."

That way, we'll both be fucked up.

See, man, most grownups ain't nothin' but some big ass kids and most kids ain't nothin' but some lil' ass adults. People who call themselves adults be some stupid muh'fuckas a lot of times. You see where the kids get it from—and that's where the humor comes from. Because you can't believe this shit!

I saw a woman trying to correct her daughter the other day. The daugher said, "I'm ain't."

The woman got mad. She said, "What'd I tell you about sayin' 'I'm ain't?' It's 'I'm isn't!' "

Then niggas try to act like they finally get an understanding of things. But it be too late.

I was at the doctor's office one day. I met this woman who was pregnant. I asked her, "So how many is that? Two?"

She said, "Naw, nine—but I ain't havin' no more."

I guess not, shit! Nine?

And we ain't even countin' the abortions. A muh'fucka got nine kids, you know she done had about four abortions.

But she wanna "get ahead in life."

People pass stupid shit on down to the kids. So the kids are in school and everybody hate the smart muh'fucka. They wanna beat him up on Friday. Muh'fucka done won the spelling bee. He spelled "philosophic," and you wanna kick his teeth out.

You remember those reading groups in school? It would be the first group, the kids who could do good. The second group was kids who were OK. Then there was that third group.

The third group was that muh'fucka who had to put his fingers on the words. The teacher gotta read with that nigga so he can get through it:

> STUDENT: Uh, "He . . . s-s-s—"
> TEACHER: "Said!"
> STUDENT: Uh . . . "said . . . th-th-—"
> TEACHER: "That!"
> STUDENT: Oh, yeah. "That."

Nigga, you got a fourth-grade education and you stutter! But you tellin' your woman, "Heh-heh, our cheese is gonna come in, baby! Don't worry 'bout it. I'm gettin' mine."

But you puttin' down the guy next door 'cause he talks proper: "Baby, l-l-l-listen to that muh'fucka. Ha ha. Ol'-ol'-ol' white talkin' m-m-m-muh'fucka."

Me? I was a pretty good student in school, and I wasn't afraid to humbug with no muh'fucka. So the niggas got me, too, but it took more than one. I balled my fist up. That meant that four of them muh'fuckas would get my ass. They in school all tough until they know you'll fight. That's when niggas would be talkin' that French shit: *"We* gon' get this motherfucka."

Man, I'll tell you: Niggas are funny. We go over the top with shit. Whatever is in, we gotta be trendy, too.

Like these names nowadays. You look at the names from generation to generation. Our names used to be simple: "Betty," "Cynthia," "Lamont."

Then *Roots* came out, and niggas lost they mind. "Zaqueeda."

Now they tryin' to be all superficial with names: "Paradise." "Alize." "Porsche." "Lexus." We get too buffoonish with that shit. You'll fuck a kid's head up with that bullshit.

We go over the top with shit. Like with the tattoos and the earrings. I'm sick of tattoos! You know how some muh'fucka got a problem with smoking? I'm like that with tattoos.

Niggas be havin' tattoos on they throat and wrist, on they belly. Tongue pierced. Eyelid pierced. On the ankle. In the crack of they ass. Then your child has to say, "This is my mother."

Just over the top. Like these niggas with cell phones. Muh'fuckas got cellular phones and no education. Muh'fucka got no job, but he got a cell phone—for a month. He in the mall, at the show, talkin' on that muh'fucka. I've even seen cats at *my* show on the phone.

CONCERT GOER: Hello? Yeah, man, motherfucka on-stage now. Yeah, he clean than a muh'fucka. What aisle you in?

But one thing about black folks: We smart when it comes to some ol' bullshit. Whatever man make, a nigga can break. Slick. Hustlers.

We can't take orders, though. On the job 9 to 5? We can't work no 9 to 5. We come in late. You supposed to start at 6:30, but if you come in 6:37, to us, you ain't late.

BLACK EMPLOYEE: I *know* you ain't tripping over 7 minutes.

But you been coming in late for the last three months! Then you'll tell on somebody else in a minute.

BLACK EMPLOYEE: Ain't this a bitch!? You gon' trip on me, because I done came in late, *but your boy Sam over there* come in late every muthafucking time, and you don't say nothin'!

And we always talking about what we gon' do on the job.

BLACK EMPLOYEEE: I'll blow this muthafucka up!

You ain't never known a black terrorist in your life! You ain't never known no black man with no nitroglycerin or no dynamite. First of all, where they gon' buy the dynamite from? When he go in to purchase it, he goin' straight to jail.

BLACK EMPLOYEE: Gimme four sticks of dynamite!
DYNAMITE SALESMAN (picking up the phone): Mutha-fucka, hold on.

He on the phone calling the police. You're going to jail.

But that's how we do. When it come to picking up the pay-check? That muh'fuckin' check better be there.

>BLACK EMPLOYEE: I'm here to pick up my check. What?
>What do you mean you don't see it, muh'fucka?

That's when we back up and start talking shit. But we don't just talk to the person we should be talking to. We gotta turn around and look at everybody in the room and talk to them, too.

>BLACK EMPLOYEE: You see this shit? He don't know, do
>he? Somebody better talk to them motherfuckers! I
>know they gon' find *mine!* I'm going to use the phone.
>Hey, man, you tell 'em: When I come back, they betta
>have my muh'fuckin' check—or I'll blow this mother-
>fucker up! It'll be a parking lot!

Another thing. Even after we do work hard, we don't enjoy life like we should. Not even after we get old. When we had grandpar-ents—*real* grandparents, not these young muh'fuckas who had kids when they was little—they didn't really know how to enjoy their re-tirement because they didn't know what to do. When you see white folks retire, they truly *retire.* They go get them a summer home. They go down where there's a warm climate. They fish every day.

Us, we get old, we don't go *nowhere.* When black folks retire, we go hang out at the barbershop. We go get another job. One day the nigga done retired from the plant, the next day that sum'bitch working as a janitor down at the bus depot or something.

I think back to Vietnam, when black and white issues were strong in this country. Blacks couldn't do this or that. We was janitors, couldn't do nothing. Those days are over. We had those days to have these days. You can't keep bringing up the past, that we've been oppressed. Every ethnic group that you can think of was slaves, if you do your history. Orientals were slaves. Indians, Mexicans. Look at the Israelites. Look at the Egyptians. They had them on posts, whipping them. Throwing salt on their backs. They was rowing and shit.

But everytime we talk, "We been oppressed!" Let it go. Don't nobody want to hear that bullshit.

We act like we want to talk about the past. Shit, let me talk about something from the 70s, and see what people say.

> ME: Man, I had a pair of platform shoes and a Cadillac back in the day. I used to be killin' 'em, boy . . .

You gon' be like, "Man, let it go! Talk about something else. It's 2001, and you still talking that '74 *bullshit.*"

See, we got two sets of rules. Rules for us and rules for somebody else. Blacks think we the only ones on this earth. White folks and us. Straight up. We don't say shit about the Orientals. If I was Chinese, I'd be mad than a mutha.

"They, ahh, don't nevah say nof'ing 'bout us! Nevah!"

Ain't no A-rabs, ain't no Russians, ain't no Germans. Ain't nothing but black and white. All you hear is black and white issues. You don't see no Chinese channels on TV, and you don't see no Chinese actors.

Hispanics? They don't got nothing. They give you that one Mexicans channel. And everybody ain't got cable.

You don't see in the movies, "Starring Hector Merero." Naw, he ain't starring in a motherfuckin' thing. Ain't no fruit stand in it.

One lady asked me in an interview, "Would you date outside your race?"

I . . . don't . . . know! I never have, but I don't know. If I like her, shit, I probably would. I can't say what tomorrow bring. If something unfortunate was to happen to me and Rhonda, I don't know. Shit, if the woman is Asian and I fall in love with her ass— I fall in love with Ping Pong—fine. I can't say. I probably would. I ain't into that. People talk about things that have happened, but those are isolated incidents. Those are isolated incidents. What that got to do with me falling in love? That's apples and oranges.

"Oh, they dragged a nigga down in Texas, so I can't marry no Filipino. Ain't no need in me messing with you."

She's like, "We been oppressed, too. We were sold—for rice!"

Black folks were oppressed, yeah, but we have to get past that. We got enough millionaires now, we can start our own businesses, our own networks, something of quality, substance. We got cats making $20 million a movie. We getting back end. We can put together our own independent films. We can buy our own doggone station now, have black soap operas.

But who gon' run it? Who gon' be in charge? That's where the fight gon' start. "I been doing this 30 years, you ain't gon' tell me—"

"I don't know what you talking about! Your day is over! You had your day. Nigga! That old shit you talking nigga, 'Up with Hope. Down with dope.' Get an apple, hope you choke! Ain't nobody going for that bullshit.

"Martin Luther King? Sick of that dream! Can't nobody else have no muthafucking dream? That's why they called it a dream. He woke up!"

Chapter Three

Entertainment

I'm watching the U.S. Open golf tournament the other day, and I'm tripping on all the people who are standing on the side watching. Muh'fuckas are just lined up in the crowd lookin' at these cats hit the ball. Somebody hits the ball—*whack*—and they go, "Ooooo . . . Ahhh . . ."

I'm waitin' on somebody to hit the ball like a regular human being.

Because somebody's going to get fucked up.

See, white folks are something else. They're all standing out there with their heads poked out. I want to see somebody get fucked up. To teach them white folks to keep they heads inside.

I'd knock somebody upside the head. Bust 'em right in the scalp. It'll look like their toupee is hanging off.

I can hear people talking 'bout, "Bernie Mac is hitting! Get back! Get back!"

All you'd hear is me hittin' the ball . . . *whack*.

And then . . . Pow! *"Ahhhhhh!"* "Call the ambulance!"

Man, mark my words: one day, somebody is gon' get fucked up standing out there. They're too close. I've seen pitchers get hit by balls. I've seen the football slip out the quarterback's hand. These athletes are great, but they are human.

But these golf muh'fuckas ain't gon' be satisfied until somebody gets hurt.

And I bet it'll be a black person who gets fucked up. They come, doing like them white folks and stick their head out. Watch it's gonna be a minority.

That white ball gon' find one of them. It'll put yo' eye out.

I can't fuck with a lot of the athletes today. A lot of them have the talent, but they don't put in the work. They aren't trying to match up to the legacy of the older greats. They more concerned with makin' money or being famous.

One of the bigger disappointments in sports has to be Mike Tyson. Mike's my man, but he never did realize all the potential he had. That was because he was more concerned with being a bully than with being one of the greats of his division. Anybody who stood up to Tyson, who wasn't afraid of him, beat his ass. From Buster Douglas to Evander Holyfield, twice. Holyfield matched up with him too damn good. He couldn't intimidate Holyfield. Plus, Holyfield hit his ass back.

In my neighborhood, Mickey was a bad ass sum'bitch. You'd be on the corner talkin': "Oh yeah, man, that's—uh-oh, here come Mickey."

E'erybody just walk off.

That's when Mickey call ya.

"Mac! Mac!"

You play like you don't hear that motherfucka. You just kept on walkin'.

"Man, don't let . . . Come here, Mac!"

Bernie Mac performing at the Kings of Comedy.

Kept on walkin'.

Then he caught me. I was goin' to the store. He came 'round the corner.

"Didn't you hear me callin' you?"

I said, "N-n-naw, man, I-I-I ain't h-h-hear you call me. Y-y-you was callin' me? If-if-if you was callin' me, I woulda came." I turned to my friend: "D-d-did you hear that he was callin' me?"

He said, "I heard when he was callin' ya."

"W-w-well, why you ain't say nothin'? You ain't *say* nothin'." I'm gettin' mad at *him*.

"I ain't know. I thought you heard him."

That's how Tyson was. He used to scare the shit outta people. Then when he got with all those other brothers . . .

But it's not like Don King messed him up. He messed himself up. He's a grown damn man. That's something we gotta get out of, too. Quit blaming every damn body. "Awww, poor thang."

What the fuck you mean "poor thang"? He done made over a $100 million. "Poor thang?" I can't feel sorry for somebody that made over $100 million. A grown-ass man.

I believe in letting the young brothers have their day in sports. I have my opinion, then I have my respect. It's their time, but I think they lack a lot of sportsmanship. I think they lack a lot of the fundamentals. They can shoot three-pointers and hang on the rim, but they can't shoot free-throws. They miss more open shots than I've ever seen in my life. And they can't lay the ball off the glass. When brothers my age was playing ball, we was playing in our panties. Shorts be so damned tight your balls used to be separated—one ball on this side, the other one on that side. It was like we had on hot pants.

Now, these niggas got to have the long shirt, the long shorts. Out there playin' in they pajamas, and still ain't got game.

*　　*　　*

We had style. We was hooping with our naturals. That's what they trying to do today: they trying to wear naturals, but they afros ain't shaped. Our shit used to be shaped.

And when we played, we played defense. It was physical. I was physical before physical came out. That's how your game got better. Especially on the playground, man, when you started bumping and grinding. If a cat elbowed you, it was "Hey, man, watch your 'bow."

Then the arguing would start. "You 'bowed me!"

"You 'bowed me! I ain't gon' let you move!"

"You 'bowed me in the chest, I ain't say a got-damned thang, nigga!"

"Nigga, I'm just telling you."

That's how it was, that was trash talking on the courts. You know you 'bowed a cat. When you came back down, he 'bowed you back. It was fair game. You know, if a brother pushed you off, it was all good.

Now, they fight about any damned thing. But the thing is, they *don't* fight—not for real.

Don't nobody hit nobody.

I done seen more misses in a humbug in the NBA than ever in my life. I remember when Alonzo Mourning got into the fight with Larry Johnson during the Heat–Knicks playoff game a few years ago. Everybody all upset—and they just wailin'.

And ain't nobody hitting no damned body.

Tracey McGrady got into a fight in the playoffs with some guy. He pushed the guy, then swung and missed him by two feet. Then them two niggas gon' fall down and start rolling on the ground, tryin' to wrestle.

Shit, I'd rather watch the WWF.

And baseball? These ballplayers today ain't shit. A motherfucker steal 20 bases, they call him a "threat." Lou Brock stole 100 bases, man! These motherfuckers don't even steal 50. Or if you hit

20 home runs and 73 RBIs, motherfuckers are like, "Man, you gotta pitch *around* that sum'bitch!"

If it's not that, then it's going too far the other way. Some of these sorry motherfuckers today got 90 home runs, 204 RBIs. What are they doing? Pitching underhanded to these motherfuckas?

I want to say something to the young athletes who may be readin' this book:

Whatever you do, don't play for the Chicago Bulls!

Fuck the Bulls.

That fat muh'fucka Reinsdorf broke up one of the best teams ever. They did Phil Jackson wrong. Did Mike wrong. No way Phil should be in Los Angeles, or Michael Jordan a fuckin' Washington Wizard.

If I was a young player and the Bulls drafted me, I'd never play for them. Draft me, I'd go back to school on they ass. And if I can't re-enroll, nigga, I'll join the Army.

Fuck the Bulls.

I was watchin' the basketball finals between Philadelphia and LA. I like that muh'fuckin' Iverson, man. He got heart, same way Jordan did. And the other teams do him like Jordan. They knock him around and shit, foul him even when he ain't got the ball.

The Detroit Pistons used to do Jordan like that all the time. They used to beat Jordan's ass. They took that nigga to the bridge every time he touched the ball! They ain't give a fuck who was open.

One time they tackled his ass. All of them just rushed him. He shot the ball, made it, but he couldn't even shoot the free throw. Rodman had stepped on his fingers. Isaiah beat him. Mahorn threw him down. Laimbeer sat on him. And Vinne Johnson's ugly ass was lookin' at him.

Aw, man, Detroit was rough.

*　　*　　*

I like Shaq's game, too. People are always sayin', "Well, he just does that because he's big."

So? Shaq can't help it that he's big. He's playin' like a big strong muh'fucka is supposed to play: Knock the fuck outta ya. 'Bow you in the mouth. Make you bite ya tongue. Put yo' eye out.

He's lettin' you know: Any time you put your hands on me, I'm coming around with my fist balled.

They say all he do is dunk. So what? You be under that basket Shaq gon' bust yo' got-damn lip.

Pete Rose, now that was one tough sum'bitch. That's the kinda ballplayer I like. That sum'bitch, he was no joke. Charlie Hustle. He know he had to be the one to start that sliding head first, diving on your stomach.

I dug Pete Rose—and I fucked myself up trying to do that shit.

I was playin' in a softball game, and caught myself tryin' to steal second. Burned my chest *up* trying to dive on my got-damn stomach.

You ever seen a black muh'fucka with a pink chest?

I burnt *all* the skin off my ass. I said, "From now on, tag me out."

I'm not diving no muthafuckin' more. I'm out. Shit, game after that, I was running to third base. The ball got there. I was undecided as to whether I was gonna slide. Before he could even tag me, I says, "I'm out." Slide? Fuck that!

Man, skin was all off this sum'bitch. I'm sitting there that night, pouring peroxide onto my chest. Man, all this shit on my chest was all white, like snow. Tryin' to slide, watchin' Pete Rose.

Now tell me he don't belong in the Hall of Fame.

These sportscasters today get on my nerves, too. I mean, I know it's what the audience wants, all this hip hop, but these sportscasters just go overboard. A muh'fucka hit a jumpshot on ESPN and it's, "Oops, upside ya head—bang, bang, ya dead."

Muh'fucka, sit yo' ass down.

*   *   *

I'm not jealous by nature. I'm just not. I don't have envy toward anybody for shit they got. I'm focused on me. And most of my life, I was always like that.

Except for when it came to that got-damn Marvin Gaye.

Man, Marvin Gaye. I was jealous of Marvin Gaye. I have to really be honest. I was jealous of Marvin Gaye. Because Marvin had what I wanted. I wished I had the charisma, the magic that he had with his fans. And I was an aspiring entertainer then.

Marvin Gaye would come out on stage: "Hey, what's happening?" They said he was a sissy, all that shit—but that muthafucka was smooth, man. "Hey, what's happening? Distant love . . ."

Aw, man. You be sitting there, trying to hold tight, all the women be screaming. You all mad, but you tryin' not to let nobody see it. You got yo' face all frowned up and shit.

See, back then, we hid our jealousy. You'd be jealous as hell, you be doing just rocking in your seat, poppin' your fingers, actin' like you into it, but you frownin' like a muh'fucka.

Your girl be going, "Ohhh! Ahhhh!"

You mad as hell, but you keep snapping your fingers and grittin' your teeth and you go, "Yeah, he jammin'."

Then Marvin hit that note. *"Wooo-Hooooooooooo!"* He be holdin' that shit! His process be sticking out a little bit!

And he be high than a motherfucker! Marvin Gaye used to be *hiiiiiiiigh.*

And yo' jealous ass, that's the only thing you can say about him, so you turn to your girl and be like: "Man, he fucked up!" And hope that just scared somebody.

Your girl just say, "That's all right, but he jammin', though! *Go 'head on, Marvin, with yo' high ass!"*

That make you even madder.

"Hmph. He probably on some . . . some her'on!" Trying to make it

DEBORAH A. BUSH, DA BUSH PHOTOS

Backstage with the Commodores.

harder than what it is: "Look at him, he look like he about to fall out! Fucker!"

That's when Marvin'd say, "I'm going to sing one more for y'all."

Your girlfriend: *"Sing one more, Marvin!"*

Here you go: "Why don't you go up there with the muthafucka then, you know? Why don't you let him to take your ass home?"

"Aw, everytime we go out you starting some bullshit. You be jealous!"

I *was* jealous, man.

* * *

It was the same thing with Michael Jackson. He was nice-looking when he was a boy. All of the Jackson family, they were a nice-looking family. And every brother was jealous of the Jackson 5. You's a damn lie. You was, too.

The Jackson 5 would come out, be jammin' like a sum'bitch.

And I'd have that same jealous face. You know that look mixed with a smile and a frown? Niggas be listening to Jeffrey Osborne, muh'fuckas like that. "Oh, they bad!" And you have that face, tryin' to smile like you ain't jealous, talkin' through your teeth, like, "Yeah, heh-heh. They bad. They bad."

Knowin' you jealous as hell.

Back in the day, they had lyrics. They sang about something. They didn't just talk about themselves. They started with love songs. It was, "Baby, I miss you. I need you back." With the bands and the instruments, it was entertaining.

When you went to a show and you saw Earth, Wind & Fire! People be sitting there, talking, "Blah-blah . . . When the show gon' start? . . . Blah-blah." Then that curtain came up! The music started! It was smoke and shit, powder'd be flying over your head.

If you was smokin' a joint, you'd be done fell out.

See, that was fun. Wasn't nobody shooting and shit, man. You were entertained. When you heard that music! Oh, man!

You got you some pussy that night!

You got you some *good* pussy that night. After the show, you went and got some chicken and got a room. And she gave you some pussy. Now we call that sympathy pussy.

> HER: I really want to thank you for tonight.
> HIM: Yeah? You had a good time?

They lookin' at each other. Then she just flop over on you, don't say a word, and motherfucker start tongue-kissin' and shit.

Muh'fuckas fuckin' to music today don't even kiss or get intimate no more. They leave the show, go get a room, and when they fuck, they fuck with their clothes on! They just pull out, pull one leg out the pants. Shirt still be on and shit. You see deodorant stains under their arms.

That's the difference between today and back then.

When they come out nowadays, most performers don't even entertain. They sing two, three songs, and it's, "Good night, good night!" and then they break the microphone. *Pow!*

You be sitting there: "This bitch ain't shit."

And they be lip-syncing, too. And the next thing you know, the record start skipping. "Hello, baby! Baby-baby-baby-baby . . ."

You be sitting up there: "That sumbitch hoarse, she must be high or something. She ain't singing!"

Old entertainers, man. I'll give you a perfect example. I was on a show and on the bill was also the Intruders. I was young when they were out, with that song "I'll Always Love My Mama." They could jam.

One night, I'm doing the show, and I was backstage with them. The lead singer was real sick. Sick as a dog. Throwin' up and shit. And they was doing their little steps and singing: *"Whodoopwhodoo-dooo . . ."* They steppin' and spinnin' and doin' their whole routine. And I mean, they were *doing* that shit, right? And as soon as they marched off stage, the lead singer bent over and—*blwwwwaaappp*—just threw up right there on the spot.

Man, and I ain't lyin', that muh'fucka just spit, wiped his mouth off, and was right back in line as they came back on that muh'fucka!

He ain't miss a beat. He just went back on, *"Doo-doop! Doo-doop! Doo-doop!"* They was doing that shit, right? and they started marching off again. The lead singer was still doing his thing, stepped, spun around in his little, circle, *"Doo-doo! Doo-doo, doo-doo!"*

I said, "Man!" Now, that was how the old school used to do it. They were real entertainers, and they gave you a show no matter what.

I know rap is the hot thang right now, but I'm a jazz man. I am not a rap person. I ain't knocking rap. But you get your average black kid and white kid, they don't want to be a doctor, lawyer, chemist. All of them, when I do a seminar and ask, "What do you want to be?" say they want to be a rapper.

Because they think it's easy. Because you ain't got to be great, all you got to do is pick out a song and talk over it. And they see what cats get. Cats get four or five million dollars, man, riding around in a Bentley with braids and gym shoes.

You don't drive no fucking Bentley with gym shoes on, okay? If you're going to be a millionaire, you got to *act* like a millionaire. You don't come out in no Bentley or no Rolls, man, with your scarf on your head and your hair braided and your tongue pierced and in no gym shoes. I'm sorry, that ain't no put-down, I'm just putting you where you belong.

That ain't nothing but some nigga shit.

Get you a Lexus or something because you messing up the traditions, man.

You a millionaire got-damnit; you're supposed to walk like a millionaire! Man, when you come out the door, you're supposed to be clean from head to toe. Naw, I'm sorry. You give a millionaire a whole new name. You keeping it real? That ain't real, dog. That's ghetto like a muthafucka.

A millionaire, you can smell him when he leaves the room. You got to put some C-L on your A-S-S, man.

Music when I was coming up, man, those were the good old days. I used to go see the Ohio Players: *"Aw, girl. If you want to listen to what people say behind my back . . . You'll be making love to me, alright! . . .*

Gimme me an L and an O got a V and an E . . ." They'd be jamming. Parliament. Bootsy. That was funkin'.

And they gave a *show*. Bootsy had the binocular glasses on, the knickerbockers, the big-ass shoes with the curve on the toe. And the smoke and fire. Rick James, Earth, Wind and Fire—that was entertainment.

They were creative with the songs. The way music is today, you got the bottom and the top. Right now it's at the bottom. There's no creativity now because the new jacks just take old shit and reuse that.

Kids don't know. They trip me out. They hear a new song on the radio, and they they be like, "Oh, that's 'Elbow!' He got a new one out?"

That ain't no muthafucking 'Elbow'! That's Smokey Robinson!

I tell my nieces and nephews, "That's the same song! Let me go get my LPs!"

When I play the song, they just be lookin'. They be in silence.

Then they go: "But I like the new one better, though."

How you gon' like somebody unoriginal shit better than the original? How you gon' do that? He stole it from him! All you hear is remakes: *When I'm riding through the alley with my gat in my hand/And I had four women, you understand. Bitch is dead/muthafucka kill 'em, shoot 'em dealing with Fred/I told him that he'd be dead.*

Naw, man. Naw, man. How you gon' dance to that when you get 70? (If you make 70.) You'll be toothless, still cussin', talkin' to your grandkids: "That muthafucka there was the jam!"

Naw, man.

I'm not a a big fan of the music today, but one thing's for sure: I'm not one of those people who blames music for everything. People are always sayin' that music made their kids do wrong.

Bullshit, man.

I don't think anybody can influence your child except for you.

Your responsibilities are yours. My grandmother used to say, when you act a certain way when you're outside, it's a reflection of your home.

You can put it on Snoop if you want to—but Snoop ain't got a damn thing to do with your crib. His video ain't but two minutes long.

So if something's wrong with your child, something was wrong from the get-go. If the people in your home ain't shit, you ain't gon' be shit. People want to censor this and change that or put a sticker on this.

Man, put a sticker on ya mama. She's raisin' you.

I still love comedy, and not just as a performer. I love to laugh, to be entertained. But speaking just as a comedy fan, not as a comedian, I don't really like a lot of what I see. They want everything fast, quick. They're just in it for the money.

They don't have the proper training. They just accept whatever. They don't commit themselves to the joke. They want something right away because cable TV has destroyed the comedy system. There's no more comedy club where you could get the basics. Comedy owners had control. They told what you could and could not do. You couldn't mimic. You couldn't steal; you couldn't copycat a motherfucker—or they put your ass in the back of the line, and they wouldn't hire you.

Now, they comedy at McDonald's, Burger King, I Fry Kingdom, Kentucky Fried Chicken. A motherfucker goes up there and talks about somebody's mama. People ain't payin' they money to be humiliated. They don't know how to host. They don't know how to MC.

Comedy clubs provided the right training. Those things are gone. People don't really go to comedy clubs. They turn on BET. They turn on Comic View. They get the raw image. So now they think, "Hey, that motherfucker is doing it. I can do it. I can go out and talk about a sum'bitch all night, and I can get paid. That's not comedy. Comedy comes from the heart and from the soul. You have to know what comedy is. You can learn to tell a joke. But being funny comes from inside. Everybody can tell a joke. Everybody can't tell a story. A storyteller is someone with imagination, someone who has range. This motherfucker ain't sittin' up here perpetrating a fraud, going up there listening to somebody else, and then going across the street and re-telling a joke you already heard.

But when you're a comic and those sum'bitches don't laugh? You ass out! And that's the difference between then and now. They don't want to pay their dues.

Bernie joins the band on the Midnight Mac Show.

You got to pay your dues. It's no different than if you gotta take a bullet outta somebody's ass on a Saturday night. You lucked up and took that motherfucker out with some pliers. Now they want to call you a doctor?

One thing comics do that I don't like is, they pick people out of the audience and make their act about that person.

People who did do that who were great were people like Don Rickles and Robin Harris. Some cat imitating them might pick you out of the audience, "Look at this muthafucka, he . . ." And you got your woman with you. See, Don and Robin didn't do that. They say, "Hey, man, your head is like a question mark. You should be at the end of a sentence." And you start laughing with him because he had a certain look on his face that described that it was all love. He made you part of the show, so to speak. He didn't try to damage you.

But now? You got your girl with you for the first night and you trying to impress her and some sum'bitch talk about you? You know, how one arm longer than the other one. You know, you sitting up there—you got cerebral palsey, your mouth twisted, your shit just now straightening up. Your girl, only reason she out with you is you got a little money. You sitting up there gettin' talked about. You want to square up on him and fight, but you know one leg is longer than the other. You walking all off balance and shit. Only reason you sit in the front row is you can't see from the back, you know.

And you a comic and you want to eat him up? Naw, I don't believe in that.

Not that I couldn't do it, you understand.

I like Eddie Murphy. I think he's the most talented sum'bitch when he ain't into himself. Like when he did *Raw*. It was the glove and diamond on the glove. I think he lost a few muh'fuckas with that.

But if I had to see somebody who can do standup, I think it would be Eddie. The funniest comics are when they aren't into themselves. You see the best. When they aren't tryin' to be politically correct, they can be funny.

Today, I can't even watch a lot of these movies. Back in the day, it used to be Cagney, George Raft, who talk to you like, "Yeah, you double-crossed me, shee. Yeah, shee, now I gotta bump ya off . . ."

Now? If it ain't no soundtrack or explosions, the movies ain't shit. Now you gotta have a muh'fucka run up a wall, flip backwards, then that sum'bitch gotta slide on two knees shooting guns from the side.

We had some bullshit in our day too, now. A muh'fucka could pull a gun and shoot your gun out your hand. *Pow! "Ahhhh . . ."*

Man, please.

Or muh'fuckas would have his hands in his pockets and act like he had a gun and could away with. He'd stick his hand in your back and be like, "Keep walkin'. Don't look back. If you turn around, I'll let you have it."

People would be all scared and shit. "Don't shoot!" That muh'fucka ain't have shit but a comb.

Chapter Four

The Career Track

The first bomb I had was here in Chicago, when I first was starting off. The producer of the show had seen me actin' a fool at a barbecue that my mother-in-law was having. He saw me clowning and said, "Man, you funny than a muh'fucka. I got a show, and I want to put you in it."

Then, my black ass.

I went on. Two minutes into my act, I heard people in the crowd: "Get yo' black ass off, man!" "Fuck you!" "You ain't-funny sum'bitch!"

All my family was there, my in-laws, all of them. I was hurt. They were just looking at me. I just walked the fuck off the stage. I was dying the death of a pilot. My shit was going *down*, dog.

So now all that clowning and shit I was doing? You know black folks. Every time I told a joke in front of my family after that, it was, "Yeah, you should've told that joke that night, muh'fucka." "Muh'-fucka, you wastin' all yo' funny jokes here." "When you was up there, you ain't say a muh'fuckin' thang." I went through that for a *while*.

I was so afraid of a microphone after that. My confidence just left me. I was so nervous, I refused to touch a mic for months, for almost a whole year.

Eventually, I came back out of hiding. I was at the Crystal Palace on 119th and Michigan in Chicago. This dude told me he wanted to hire me for a big party.

I ain' gon' lie to you: I punked out. This is one of the most embarrassing stories I have to tell.

I got to the Crystal Palace, man, and it wasn't nothing but pimps, players, hustlers, and ho layers. I mean, it was *packed*. I'm sitting backstage, right? They got this little curtain, and I'm peeking through. Everybody's just sitting out there, talking. The room was just buzzing.

The producer of the show came back there, said, "Bernie, show time is in ten minutes."

I started breathing hard, sweating.

He came back a short while later: "Five minutes."

I walked out into the hallway, stood by some phones.

He came back by a little bit later: "Bernie, get ready to go on, man."

When he walked by, I grabbed up one of the phones and pretended like I was having a serious conversation. Soon as he said, "Get ready to go on."

I screamed into the phone, "What? I'll be right there!"

I turned to him and said, "Man, somebody done jumped on my motherfuckin' wife, man!" I started walking toward the door real fast.

He said, "Bernie! Bernie!"

I'm all loud, faking like I'm upset and shit: "Man, I gots to go take care of this shit here!"

"We'll go and help you."

I said, "Naw, man, I got it!"

And I *ran* out the motherfuckin' door, man.

I got in the car. I drove two blocks. I pulled over. I said, "You punk motherfucker." I felt this small. One, for lying; two, for not facing my fear; three, for running.

But I was frightened. I had to get the fuck outta there.

As an actor, I've had to be careful about the roles I've taken. Because I know black folks: Whatever you play, whatever you do, they take for real. Like, I played the dude Jing-A-Ling in *Life*. He was supposed to be having a relationship with another man in prison. They wanted me to play him as a flaming homosexual, but I refused. Partly because that would've been too easy.

But also 'cause I know black folks—and I didn't want no repercussions.

BLACK MOVIEGOER: You up there playing an old fag? Man, man, Bernie Mac, c'mon, man.

So I had to make Jing-A-Ling so you really didn't know he was gay. I couldn't play him flaming. Naw, 'cause brothers will beat you up. They take shit for real. They don't know it's a movie. Black folks do not understand that this is pretend—like when you little and you play house, postman and all that shit. You playing.

But black people, they be serious. We watch *The Fugitive,* and we like, "Unh-uhh, he played that *too* well! Harrison Ford probably did something like that in real life!"

Or like in *Players Club* where, at the end, my character, Dollar Bill, gets hit over the head and thrown in a trunk.

I get people come up to me even today and say, "Hey, man, where they take you in that trunk?"

Now, these are fans—so I try to be nice. But you know I be wanting to say, "You stupid muthafuckas."

This one guy asked me—and this ain't no lie—he said, "Hey, Bernie Mac! They killed you, didn't they? Man, how they be doing that?"

Bill Belamy, Laura Hayes, Michael Cuyler, and Bernie Mac, with Chris Tucker (crouching).

I just looked at him and said something. Then he said, "But they hit you with a bat! I know *that* was real!"

These muthafuckas something else; they be believing this shit. They do.

Now, I can see a little kid doing that. I got a friend, her grandson, cutest little chocolate boy you ever want to see. And he smart. He short as hell, 'bout three feet tall. Muh'fucka eight years old. He ain't growing no more, right? But he's smart.

Anyway, I went over their house and he went off: "How is Bernie Mac over here and he dead? They put him in the trunk!" He said, "Lord, what's going on here?"

Now that was funny to me because he's a little boy. But grown folks be coming to me with this bullshit—talking about, "Where Kid and Play at?

"We saw you in *House Party* last week, man. What Kid doing?"

I don't know!

Another time, I was somewhere playing golf. A brother came up to me, he said, "Bernie Mac, what's up man?"

I said, "What's up, brother? How you doing?"

Then he gon' ask me: "Where Steve Harvey and Ced at?"

Like we sleep together or something! We ain't connected at the hip, muh'fucka. I don't know.

Brothers hold you so close to everything, it's amazing. If you sing a song, you can't have imagination.

> BLACK MUSIC FAN: You heard that song about wanting to be banged? You know, listen to the words. "Oh, daddy, no, my booty sore." You know his father a fag, right?

We take things out of context. Everything is real to us.

But I don't think people care all that much about who I am. Muh'fuckas don't remember all that "he was funny" shit. They don't care about the person behind the act. They just wanna know your business.

Muh'fuckas want dirt on you. They want to hear somethin' bad.

I'm sure people talk shit about me. "That muh'fucka make me sick." Because they know I'm gonnna make it rough. They know I ain't bullshittin' when I get on that stage.

Niggas are afraid, a lot of them, because they don't work at it. I don't even know a lot of their names. Hearing the names of comedians today is like listening to the weather bureau: Earthquake, Tornado, Snowflake, Hurricane. There's Pierre and T. J. Smooth.

People come up to me and say, "Bernie Mac, Bernic Mac! I love you, man. My nephew's a comedian. Ever heard of Boxhead?"

Not a whole lot of people have gone out of their way to help me. I mean, Phyllis Hyman was truly a blessing to me. She hooked me up with my first really big gig, out at the Hollywood Bowl in LA years ago. And there have been others, too.

But there haven't been too many comics who have done a lot for me. I'd go to the amateur room and people would play me to the left. A lot of the other comics had their cliques and shit, and I wasn't really a part of all that. I mean, I was cool with a few guys, but not too much so. Hollywood was a muh'fucka. I got rejected so many times in Los Angeles.

I can go all the way back to Damon Wayons and *Mo' Money*. I had gone out for a part in the movie, but I didn't get it, right? But later, the people involved with the movie told me that they really liked my work and that Damon was going to give me a part in the movie. And this was when Damon was hot. *In Livin' Color*, his HBO comedy special, he had all that goin' on. Hot as hell.

So not long after I read for that part, I was back in Chicago hosting at the Cotton Club like I did every Monday night, and Damon came to my club. I walked in the back; he was there. We started talkin', and he told me, "All right, I'm gon' out you in my movie."

Man, don't you know, I was a *doorman* in the movie *Mo' Money*? All I did was open the door.

He's hookin' me up, right?

I don't think I said, "Uh-huh" in that muh'fucka. I ain't say, "Come in," "Please," or nothin'.

I was a *doorman!* I could've at least asked, "Who is it?"

Everytime them white folks go up there on those award shows and get their trophies, they don't never give thanks to God. Because they think they are God. They have control. They control your destiny. They sit there and they tell you if you live or die. And the blacks believe that. Hispanics and Asians, they ain't got nothing coming. And if you do get a role, you a ho. You gon' be a drug dealer. Or you gon' be a snitch.

Then you have the blacks go up there to get their awards: "First I'd like to thank God who made it possible . . . What's up, muthafuckas? What's up, yo! To the people, man. Sho' you right! Raydon, Jerky, Samuel, Lil' Wee-Wee. I'm comin' home, baby! I want to thank God, though, for real. For real!"

But in Hollywood, blacks know what we're up against, so ain't no reason to keep getting angry. How many times have we seen this? So why does it still bother us? I done seen every side of prejudice. I done went on an audition, went into a room, and ain't nothing but blacks there—for one role: Jamie.

Niggas ask you, "What you here reading for?"

"I'm reading for Jamie, nigga! *He* reading for Jamie. *She* reading for Jamie. *We all* reading for Jamie!"

"And he die in the beginning of the movie. So I hope y'all die good, whoever get the role—because you gon' be a dead mutha-fucka."

Sho' 'nuff, three minutes into the movie, Jamie dead.

JAMIE: You ain't gon' do a muthafu—

Pow!
That be your only line.

And after you done been in a movie like that, you're so embarrassed. Your friends be like, "I thought you was in the movie."

Because you know black folks ain't coming at the beginning. A fourth of the movie is over and we got to scoot past a muthafucka. "Sit down! Sit down!" "I left my coat. Excuse me one more time." "Damn!"

When we get there, we chewing all loud and shit, talking to the movie.

BLACK MOVIEGOER: What? That's stupid, muthafucka! Ain't no way I go up in that room like that! Hell naw! That's some Hell Naw!
WHITE MOVIEGOER: Shh!
BLACK MOVIEGOER: What? You don't tell me what to do! I'm grown! We can take it to the bridge!
BLACK MOVIEGOER'S GIRLFRIEND: Don't say nothing to him, baby.
BLACK MOVIEGOER: White muthafucka gon' tell *me* . . . Let me get a sip of that ice, girl. Ow!
GIRLFRIEND: You still got that hole in your tooth?
BLACK MOVIEGOER: Aw, yeah. Hey, I thought you said Jesse was in this movie?

And then when the movie ends and they don't see you, they talk about you.

> MOVIEGOER: That movie wasn't shit! Wait until I see that muthafucka. That muthafucka wasn't in no movie. That's a lying muthafucka.

But he was in it—you just missed him. He dead. When you get the movie on videotape, you see.

> MOVIEGOER: Oh! There that muthafucka! Hit stop, Frank! Frank, come here. This is it!
> *(Gets on the phone)* Hey, man, what's up, man, what you doing? Man, I got the tape. Jesse *is* in this muh'-fucka, man. I got it for $7. A man was selling it by the grocery store, bootleg. But yeah, you got a few clear spots. You can see his head . . . Oh, shit! They just shot Jesse on here! Shit just started and he dead already.
> Damn, I know that hurt. How they be doin' that?

I ain't complainin' about my success; I grew up hard, so to have the money and fame that I have achieved is all gravy. This stuff is just the cherry on top.

But that doesn't mean that everythang is cool. It's hard some-times when you've made it and people see that. People use you. They try to get stuff outta ya—especially money. I don't mind doing it for somebody I care about, but people take it too far.

They play psychological blackmail. Instead of just coming out and telling you something—"Bernie, could you help me with my rent this month?"—they throw innuendos: *"Sigh* . . . I don't know *what* I'm gon' do, man."

They want you to say, "What? What's wrong?"

I don't say nothing.

They say it a few more times: "Yeah, man . . . *sigggghhhhh* . . . I don't know *what* the fuck I'm gon' do . . . *Sigghhhh* . . . Shit's deep."

I still don't say nothing. They waiting on me to say, "Man, what's up?" But see, I learned—don't say shit.

Then they'll say it loud. "Don't make no got-damned sense, man. Shit! Pretty soon I'm gon' have to get a trailer! Man, moving gon' be a bitch! Muthafucka gon' try to put us out first thing in the morning! I ain't gon' worry about it, though."

I ain't either. I just stay quiet.

They keep goin': "Aw, man, you know, landlord *trippin'*."

I'll go onto something else: "So how ya kids?"

I'm so good, I know the bullshit when it come. The phone'll ring . . .

ME: Hello?
PITIFUL VOICE: Hello?

Bernie Mac and daughter Je'Niece at her graduation.

Soon as I hear that voice, I'm already like, "Here it come."

> ME: Hold on. You wanna speak to Rhonda?
> PITIFUL VOICE: Sighhhh. Yeah. She in?
> ME: Yeah, she's in. Hold—
> PITIFUL VOICE: How *you* doin', Bernard?
> ME: I'm doing good, good. How you doin'?
> PITIFUL VOICE: *Sigghh*. I'm blessed . . .

What the fuck you beggin' for if you so damn blessed then?

> PITIFUL VOICE: I might be blind in one eye. This arthritis
> might be killing me, but I'm blessed. I take heart pills
> and medicine, and my high blood pressure is sky high.
> But I'm blessed. My diabetes is actin' up, and my big
> toe done got an infection in it, and boy, this hyperten-
> sion keep going up and down.
>   But Lord let me see another day. I'm blessed.

If you blessed, why you cranking and moaning and bitching?

Man, more people come to me for money. Bullshit money. And they don't never pay you back. Bullshit money is if they need a thousand, I give 'em five thousand. If they need five, they come for ten. And they can't just come at you with one problem. They gotta have a whole list of bullshit.

> BEGGING BROTHER-IN-LAW: They laid me off from my
> job, man. Your niece, man, got to have an operation. I
> ain't told your sister, but I need about $8,000. I know
> you ain't gon' let your niece go through all of this, man.
> Man, we family. The only thing we got is one another.
> I'm gon' pay you back. I swear to God I'm gon' pay you

back—if I have to sell my arm or something! But I can't let my daughter die, man!

You lie on your daughter? Lie on they own *kids!* Now, I don't mind helping you, but when you get to that, you bullshittin'.

I used to be into giving people money for Christmas. I'd get my family over here and just give out checks. You know, I just wanted to keep the family thing going.

One Christmas, everybody was over. We had just got our house. People in the basement talkin', opening presents. I came downstairs, and I heard my family member talkin' about, "How much he give *you?*"

Muh'fuckas was comparing! "We got more last year, didn't we?" "Hmph . . . Muh'fucka cuttin' back."

Betcha I won't do that no mo'. I cut that out—and that was three years ago.

When I ask for the money back, it's not really that I want the money back. I just be trying to get control over the situation. Because if you don't stop them, it gets out of hand.

> **ME:** Hey, man, I thought you was gon' get that back to me? You ain't gotta do it right now, but I just want to put something on your mind.
> **BEGGING BROTHER-IN-LAW:** Oh, man, hold up now. Look here, man.

He just came crying three or four months or a year ago.

Now? He won't even call you. Won't even mention it to you. Just stop coming around. Now when you see him, he got a fucking attitude.

ME: Hey, man what's going on?

BROTHER-IN-LAW: Ain't *nothin'* going on. Hmmph.

What the fuck is he short about? He owe me money—but now he don't want to speak.

Then when you ask him for it, he throws your success at you.

ME: Hey, man, can I talk to you for a second? I thought you said you was gon' pay me back.

BROTHER-IN-LAW: Aw, that little bit of money ain't gon' hurt you, man? You sweating me on some *bullshit*, man.

ME: What?

BROTHER-IN-LAW: I'm just saying, man . . . You ain't hurting.

ME: What you saying? This is *my* money you talking about, man!

BROTHER-IN-LAW: I'm just saying . . . You got your own *TV show* and you gon' sweat me for $5,000? Man, I'm gon' *give* you your got-damned money. You ain't got to . . .

Hold on! See, that's the front. Talk all loud, try to make me feel bad.

MY SISTER: What's going on in here?

BROTHER-IN-LAW: Ask your brother! Ask your *rich-ass* brother!

They play the mind games . . .

SISTER: Bernie, what you done did?

ME: Look, all I did was ask him for my money.

SISTER: You know he got high blood pressure! And I'm your *sister!* Look here. We all slept in the same bed together. We gon' give you your *money*, Bernie. You ain't got to come over here like you our landlord.

ME: I ain't come to you like that. It's been two years.

SISTER: Fuck that! I gave you a lot of money when you ain't have nothing. When you ain't have a damn dime. Before you became "Bernie Mac"!

Now, here come the tears. Muh'fuckas tryin' to make you feel bad for doing good . . .

SISTER: We gon' *give* you your *money*. Don't *worry* about it.

BROTHER-IN-LAW: Naw, baby, naw! Fuck him!

SISTER: Naw, I can't fuck him. I'm just gon' pray for him! The Bible say that money is the root of all evil.

Ain't that some shit? They gon' quote the Bible! I said to myself, *Look at these muthafuckas.*

I just go on. I don't never get paid back. I got so much money out there, I could get me three houses. Straight up. And each one of them would be over $200,000. Personal loans, saving homes, people sayin' they going to school—and then don't go. I done helped out with all kinds of shit.

And if you do ever pay me back, knowing me, you put the money in my hand and I'll probably turn around and say, "You keep it."

I just want to see you know the principle. I don't want your money. I just want you to do what you say you gon' do. I ain't no loan officer.

If it ain't problems over the money, it's problems over a sum'bitch bein' jealous. Now like I said before, I ain't really a jealous guy. I don't get mad at other people for what they got.

But it's a whole bunch of jealous sum'bitches out there. I see 'em. They got what I call the "combo look." That's when you jealous as hell, but you try to smile like you ain't jealous. But a frown mean you jealous than a muthafucka. A muthafucka smile and frown at you, he jealous. With that combo look? That muh'fucka jealous.

Them combo looks a muh'fucka, boy. I even seen those combo looks on award shows. You can tell that muthafucka don't like that muthfucka who won. The announcer will be like, "And the winner is Denzel Washington."

You see them on the shows, clapping and trying to keep that fake smile on. Clappin', frownin', and smilin' at the same damn time. He mad than a muh'fucka.

I get niggas comin' up to me with that same bullshit. Wearin' that combo look, but be trying to act like everything cool: "Saw you on the news, Bernie man! Heh-heh. Go on and get your fo' million! Go on get your money, man . . . heh-heh . . . I ain't mad at ya!"

Sheeiiittt. He mad as hell. Bend your ass over, that muthafucka'll put a hammer to your head.

When you're successful, women got a way of gettin' yo' ass. They'll tell on you when you successful. They see you on TV or something, they gotta tell.

> WOMAN 1: Girl, Bernie Mac, I used to suck his dick. Girl, I sucked his dick right over there behind that McDonald's. Yeah, we went to the beach and everything, got us some fish sandwiches and everything.
> WOMAN 2: *Giiirrrl!* What made you do it?
> WOMAN 1: I just started sucking it, girl. I just had the motive to suck it. I sucked the shit out of him. He damn near passed out.

Now, if I'm a bum or something and she gave me some, and they see me on the corner and I'm scratching, all that kind of shit . . .

WOMAN 2: There go Bernie Mac. Didn't you used to fuck him?

WOMAN 1: Naw! Naw! Naw! Now, he *asked* me for some, but I ain't never really . . . Naw, I ain't never . . . Unh-unh.

WOMAN 2: You a lie! You *did* fuck him! You did!

WOMAN 1: Naw! Now we was *kissing*. We did *kiss*. He caught me off guard; I kissed him back. But he looked better than he do now. He looked much better than he do now.

But naw, I ain't give him none. I *almost* gave him some behind the McDonald's. But the manager came to the window, and we broke it up. I'm glad we did. But I didn't give him none.

WOMAN 2: He said you sucked his dick.

WOMAN 1: He a gotdamn lie! I ain't never . . . Unh-unh . . . Now, I *looked* at it. But I ain't sucked it. Don't be lying on me!

I'm telling you man, people are funny.

As a comedian, there are certain subjects I stay away from. Like politics. I'm not into politics. I'm not a politician. Everybody don't have a view. Some people just want to get up in the morning and live their lives with their families and mind their damn business. Everbody ain't in on current events, you know what I'm saying? But people always try to make you: "What do you think about foreign policy?"

I don't think a *got*-damn thing about foreign policy. My life is foreign as it is.

What you see is what you get. And I tell it like it is each and every day. I walk in rooms by myself. I ain't got no posse. I don't

need a bodyguard. I ain't runnin' for Congress. Man, I'm a comedian.

What the fuck I need a posse for? Who the fuck wanna assassi-
nate a comedian? That's like fuckin' wit' Bozo.

Next thing you know, it was a black thing. You had to have a
posse.

I'm the odd man out because I don't fall into what is now a tra-
dition of having 20 sum'bitches with you. I'm not that insecure. I
don't live like that. I don't like a lot of people around me because
it's trouble. Your problem become my problem. Just because I'm a
billionaire, don't mean I want to buy drinks everytime I see you.
I don't give a fuck if I got a $100 million, I don't want to buy
dinner every night. Gimme a apple. Buy me a Falstaff. Gimme a
thank-you card.

Bernie Mac and friends...

Bodyguards, groupies—see, all that's bullshit. I don't pay groupies no attention. My mentality ain't there. I see 'em, but I *don't* see 'em. Titties out. Booty out. You want me to come home to *that?* Fake mole on ya lip and shit. Hairdo this goddamn high. Tattoos every doggone where.

You ain't wearing no draws—how I'm gon' call you my broad? I don't like women who are the same. I ain't gon' call 'em a hoochie, but you're the same. You come a dime a dozen.

I see it everyday. Look on *Soul Train.* It's on the videos. Lookin' like a basketball player, tattoos all up on her arm. You look nasty. You look like you stank!

I always been a people person, and I've always had love for my fans. My fans made me, and I know it.

But some fans I just can't mess with.

Like yesterday, right? I was in my ride on my way home, and I noticed that the whole way there was this car following me. I was gettin' off the expressway at my stop and, all of a sudden, this car gon' swerve all the way over onto the shoulder.

I'm lookin' through my rearview mirror. Scared an' shit, right?

Then they pulled up on the side of me: "Hey, Bernie Mac, hey! Hey! Yeah, man, hahahahaaaaa, I love yo' shit, nigga."

I sped the fuck up.

These sum'bitches *followed* me. They were like, "Roll the window down, muh'fucka! Hahahahaah! Roll the window down!"

Man, I pulled off.

I know they talked about me like a dog. But I ain't give a fuck.

I love my fans, but I ain't givin' in to no foolishness. I love me some fans.

I don't think about them, though. You're cheating yourself. It's not those who get there first. It's those who get there and stay there the longest. I've got the patience of Job. I've been waiting a long time. I ain't been the first to do a damn thing. I know I'm going to be standing. Get off. Go ahead. I can write. I can think. I believe. I got faith. That's something a lot of them cats don't have. They want it quick. Put 'em in, bam, pop up. "I want what you got." One part is cold, one part is hot. The middle is lukewarm. Bake me! Take your time. Put me on 350, check me every now and then, make sure I pop up and *bam!* I'm Doug E. Fresh. I got the patience of Job.

I see other comics. I watch 'em. I hear 'em. I don't listen to the voices: *Ooo, he funny!* I just say okay. I ain't got nothing negative to say about nobody. I can't gain nothing beating you down to build myself up. I don't deal with toxic waste. I can show you better than I can tell you. Might take a little time, but it's gotta be seasoned.

I just look at it like I'm in training, man. So when the time comes for me, I'm ready. I'm ready. I've been in the gym. You can't stop me. I got the head weights on. I ain't soft. You can't get in here. I don't hear the voices. If I had listened to them, I'd never be where I am right now. That's their job to discourage me. That's people's job to say that. "That's all right. This is wack." That's their job. So when you listen to them, you can stop being focused and stop doing what you're doing.

> **FRIEND:** People don't front on Bernie anymore, but they used to. They didn't know how big he had become.
>
> I was with him one time when he did this show down at the Holiday Star in Chicago. The bill was featuring the O'Jays, the Whispers, and Bernie. The Whispers were supposed to go on first. Bernie was the icebreaker between all the love songs and then the O'Jays. The Whispers don't want to go on first. They want Bernie to go on first. They're like, "Why the fuck do we have to go before him? That nigga's just a comedian."

The people at the Holiday Star told the Whispers, "Y'all can take y'all muthafuckin' ass home. Bernie will fill this bitch up by himself."

BIG NIGGA: Yup, I remember that. I was there, too. The Whispers said they wasn't gon' do it. My man at the Holiday Star said, "We don't need ya."

So then, they looked out from behind the curtain, and saw all those motherfuckers out there. I mean, that place was packed—and a lot of 'em just came to see Bernie. They saw they were about to lose out on that cheese.

Next thing you know, them motherfuckers out there, spinnin' and shit, and it's, *"And the beat goes oooonnn . . ."*

Them muh'fuckas took they ass out on that stage.

When I first started putting my family into my bits, they were mad than a muthafucka: "You sitting up there telling our family business. It ain't none of their business. Everything ain't funny, Bernie."

They're mad until they see the people's reaction. Then when they see the reaction, it's, "That's me! He talking about me!"

See it's a different thang then. At first, it was, "Old black muthafucka gonna sit up there and tell our business! 'Hee-hee' my ass! You gonna have people thinking I'm crazy! I don't be doing that!"

Then they saw the people's reaction, and they changed. Like they getting some residuals or something.

People tell me I look a little different nowadays than I did when a lot of people first saw me on *Def Comedy Jam* way back when. Back then, I used to wear glasses. They was funny looking, but that's not why I wore them. I wore them because I couldn't see.

I wasn't caring about them people. You lucky I ain't come out with no dog!

* * *

What people have to say about me doesn't bother me, whether I'm on stage or off. I don't care.

And one thing I sure don't do: I don't let no heckler take me out of my show. The best way to deal with a heckler is let him take his self out. Because most hecklers want to be you. They're jealous. Most hecklers think they funny. Or they funny with their boys. Most of them have to be high in order to even try to get some attention. You got false confidence right there. They around all these people and they hollering out your name. "Go, Bernie!" Or, "Go, whoever it is!"

That just boils his ass, "Oh, this muthafucka ain't all that. Fuck that black muthafucka. Look at that old loud-ass suit. Juggle some balls, nigga! Clown-ass nigga!"

They got to put you down to build themselves up. That's what most hecklers are. But inexperienced comedians don't know how to deal with them. First of all, can't nobody hear that sumbitch but the few people around him, okay? So, if you let him keep on, they gon' kick his ass for you. Because ain't nobody pay no $30 or $40 to hear this stupid sum'bitch. So, if you talking and got the microphone and hear somebody go, *"Ohhh"* you know they done threw that muthafucka off the balcony. You let the brother hang his self.

Being successful has opened up all kinds of stuff for me. I'm doing things I never used to do.

Like I play golf a lot. I play as much as I possibly can. I got into golf about six years ago. I started watching it at first. Tiger Woods wasn't even a pro yet.

Before, an old agent of mine used to try to get me to play. I'd be like, "Man, I ain't playin' that sissy shit! I'm used to runnin' and jumpin', hoppin' the fence to chase a motherfucker and shit. That's my kind of sport!"

Man, the first time I played golf, I was tired as a muh'fucka! I was walkin' all bent down, my back hurtin', ball wasn't goin' nowhere. I'm just out there hurtin' the earth. I mean, I'm beating the ground the fuck up!

Then I got one or two good hits. That juiced me up. I started taking lessons. I started to really learn the game, what putting means, what a chip shot is. Golf ain't no chump game. It's strategic. And I ain't just playing the course. I'm also playing the elements.

Then you out there, the breeze blowing, the sun shining, the grass is nice and green. It's something a nigga ain't accustomed to.

Shit, they out there talkin' about "caddy." I ain't know what a caddy was. I said, "Man, we gon' drive a Cadillac out on this muh'-fucka?"

I've been hunting for the past few years, too. But when I hunt, I don't go for the kill. I go for the skill.

They call me "the peaceful hunter." 'Cause I ain't killed nothin' yet.

The first time I went huntin', I ain't know what the fuck I was doing. My pants were pressed. My boots were shined. I had cologne on. My pager was on my hip. I think I had a sharp hat on.

This old man who I was goin' with looked at me and said, "Where the fuck you goin'?"

He was like, "The motherfuckin' animals gon' smell your ass a mile away! We ain't gon' catch shit! You ain't onstage, muh'fucka!"

So we got to the grounds and, on the outside, there was all kinds of animals out. It was quail, raccoon, squirrel. They were runnin' around all past us.

You are entitled to three squirrels, two rabbits, two quail. And if it's quail season, then you can't shoot rabbit. You can't even load up until you get 500 feet inside the gate around the grounds.

The animals know the rules. So they runnin' past, lickin' their tongue out at you and shit. *"Nyaaah,* muh'fucka."

So we go 500 yards inside, somebody said, "Load up." We

loaded up—and you ain't see nobody. Those muh'fuckin' animals was *gone!* We walkin', stalkin'. You couldn't find them muh'fuckas. We walked for three, four hours. Muh'fuckas vanished.

This one guy out of all of us caught one quail. We were out there five, six hours. We came back, had to unload. We got from behind the gate, them deers, rabbits and shit started coming out, flying around.

I said, "Ain't this a bitch!" Them muh'fuckas was playing like it wasn't shit!

When you go hunting, the dogs are a trip. You see how those dogs hunt those game? Tails stick up. Nose stuck out. They'll go flush the rabbit. You'll hear the dogs barking. That means he runnin' him toward you.

So I'm out there, and I ain't shot shit, right? My friends say, "Okay, Bernie, this next one is your rabbit." They all beatin' my

Michael Jordan and wife Juanita Jordan attend Bernie Mac's weekly Tuesday night show in Chicago in 1995.

balls and shit. Then they said, "Get ready!" The dog was howling. The rabbit came out the bushes. He looked at me.

Everybody's screaming, "Shoot it! Shoot it!"

I raised up. The rabbit started running. I ain't do nothin'.

The dog came out the bushes and snapped at my ass: "Muh'-fucka! All that work I'm doin' and you ain't shootin' shit!"

Man, niggas was so mad at me, on the way home, they put me in the back with the dog.

The dog was in my ear growling all the way: "Black ass mother-fucka! Christian-ass muh'fuckin' hunter, lettin' rabbits and squir-rels go by like they payin' a toll!"

'Round here, muh'fuckas come all in your house, walk around your shit like Bro'man on *Martin*. You havin' a cookout, and he just show up. A muh'fucka will be sittin' in your backyard smokin' cig-arettes. He don't be a neighbor or nothin'.

He just smelled barbecue and came on in.

I don't know this motherfucka! And he ain't bringin' nothing either? Fuck him!

You don't even know the muh'fucka, but he walk in and grab a drink. Start dancing with your mother-in-law. He grindin' all on her. Your father-in-law's mad: "You know that muh'fucka? Well, you better get his ass." The nigga just be in ya house, slow dancing with your daughter and shit.

Now, you can't just shoot a muh'fucka for no reason. You only shoot people for certain things:

1) for fucking with your daughter
2) for comin' into your barbecue, and
3) for being in your garage fuckin' with your tools.

You need good reasons. A muh'fucka fuckin' your daughter? He supposed to get shot.

*   *   *

You only tell certain muh'fuckas that you gon' shoot 'em.

You drinkin' and arguing with a nigga. He's bigger than you. You like, "What? Man, you fuck around, get shot fuckin' with me."

You scared. You ain't gon' shoot nobody.

You know, some niggas just gotta tell you they gon' shoot you so they won't look like a coward and shit.

"Man, move your car!"

"What? Nigga, don't . . . Man, I'm gon' move it so I won't have to shoot yo' ass!"

A nigga dancin' with your woman: "That's my woman, nigga!"

"Man, you better get the fuck outta here before I beat your ass."

(Sigh.) "Man, let me go on before I have to shoot me a mother-fucka up in here!"

Naw, you ain't gon' shoot nobody. You just scared.

And I'm not sayin' you should shoot anybody. But you should be able to protect yourself.

Another good thing I've been doing is working out more. I was always athletic, but I got older and just kinda got distracted. So now, I got a personal trainer, and I'm getting myself in good shape, physically and mentally.

I go to the gym, but I hate to work out with other people. I like to exercise by myself. I'm focused. I like to get in and get out. Too many other muh'fuckas like to talk.

I'm liftin' 200 pounds and a muh'fucka wan' ask me a damn question. "Hey, man, how's Eddie Murphy?"

I'm on my fifth rep and shit, and a muh'fucka come over: "Can you sign this?"

Muh'fuckas be watching you and shit, too, man. I hear 'em: "He can't lift 15 pounds, that weak muh'fucka." "How much weight was on there? 125? He took it all off." "How much on there now?" "Sixteen pounds." "Talkin' 'bout he goin' for *reps.*"

* * *

I love comedy—but it's gonna be a day when I say, "You know what? Gotta move on." There's only so much you can talk about. I think you reach your peak. It's no different than Ali. It's no different than Bill Cosby. They don't sell tickets like they used to.

Man, in 10, 15 years, the world gonna be so different. They already got that virtual reality. I'll be 55, 60 years old, "W-w-w . . . I ain't scared of you, muthafuckas." Niggas'll be saying, "Look at that bald head muthafucka. Man, he's through!"

I don't wanna go out like that. I want you to always remember me as being one of the best. Not as some old nigga who can't quit: "I'm coming back! Gimme my cane over there, Jordan! I'm coming back like a muthafucka. I might not be able to play power forward, but I'll play the two."

I'm not being foolish. When that time comes, I can ride off into the sunset, me and Rhonda. And feel good about myself, knowing I gave 150%. I'm going out on top.

Chapter Five

Family

It's funny: People always want what you got. They look at me now and say they don't see me having any pressure. That's because I went through all of it. They don't think me and Rhonda ever had our differences. We don't have any differences—now. Now, we're beyond all of that.

But, man, we had some humbugs. Physical.

That muh'fucka would come at you like Joe Frazier—head down, just swinging.

One time we had a humbug, she had said, "You ain't going out." I had went out two days in a row, coming in four, five o'clock. She gon' say, "I done told you about daylight hitting you, didn't I?"

You don't tell me what to do. I'm grown. So I said, "I'm gonna show you how grown I am."

She said, "You ain't going nowhere today."

"Who you talking to? Yeah, OK."

I tried to go to bed. My head was sore! Beating like a heart! I was out drinking with the boys. So I get in the bed. And she turn the radio on real loud! Then she let the blinds up, gon' open the drapes. The sun was beaming in on me, my head was hurting.

She said, "You won't get no muthafucking rest tonight, I bet you that. I bet you won't get no rest today. You should've got some rest where you was."

My daughter, her nickname is Boots, she gets up out of the bed. So I got to cool out.

Meanwhile, Rhonda making breakfast for everybody—except me. The house smell all good. I walk in the kitchen and ain't shit for me to eat.

How the fuck you cook just *two* chicken wings? Everybody eating *but* you.

I ask my daughter, "Boots, can I have some?"

She like, "Daddy, this all she cooked!"

So anyway, 'round five or six o'clock, I got a call. My buddy's like, "*Blaseblah*, c'mon, man, we goin' out."

I said, "Uh, I'm in. Shit, I'm in!"

My wife heard me on the phone. She said, "Didn't I tell you, I say you ain't going nowhere tonight?"

I told her, "Man, you don't tell me what to do. Watch and see!"

I put my clothes out, laid them across the bed and everything. I had my draws on the side, my "go-out" draws. You know, those the ones that be in the crack of your ass. Where you take them off at night and they got a little brown stain on the rim. Little doo-doo on the rim. You can't help it with all that sweating and dancing. I don't care how much you wash and scrub, you still gon' end up with a brown line in your draws. A number "1." A "1" or an "11." You got a "111" in your draws you done shitted.

So I'm sitting up there, she walked in, and she said, "You got your good draws out!"

I got my cologne, I'm spraying my draws down and everything, you know. I'm clean shaven, hair all even.

She said, "You come back up in here, it's gon' be some shit. I'm telling you now."

I said, "Well, I'm not worried about it. You got to bring it."

So I ain't sweating nothing, right? I come in the house six o'clock in the morning.

Man, that sister met me at the door with a slip on and had a scarf on her head with a knot like Aunt Jemima—like she was making some pancakes.

I walked in. Then, all of sudden, she was *behind* the door.

And she pushed the door back. She had her hand behind her back. She said, "You think I'm bullshitting, don't you?"

I said, "Look . . ."

Meanwhile, I'm lookin' all behind her back trying to find her hand. I had to look to find her hand.

I said, "Look here. L-l-look."

See, you know when you're nervous, when you say shit like, "Hey, hey, *hey! Hey!*"

She said, "Muthafucka, I done told you."

"Looka here," I said. "Look here."

She said, "No, I'mma cut your ass in two."

"Lemme tell ya something—not if you're hurt first!"

Next thing you know . . .

Aaagghghh . . . Boom . . . Crash . . . Agggh . . . Huaahhh . . . Aaaahhh. . . .

My daughter come out: "They fighting! They fighting!"

"Go back in the room, baby!"

My wife biting me on the side. I gotta announce it: "Ah, this muthafucka biting me!"

Man, we scrapping. Scrapping! I'm elbowing her in the neck. She hollering. I got that cranium. That 'bow hit that cranium—*pow!*

She hollerin': *"Ahhh-oh,* you done fucked up now! You done fucked up *now!"*

She went and got a hammer.

Oh, man, she hit me on the side of the head with that hammer. And she said, "Thor! Thor! I'mma Thor your ass!"

Man, I had a speed knot on the side of my muthafucking head so big, it was sticking out like a sprung thumb.

The neighbors called the police. Now I heard a knock on the door—*bam bam bam.*

Aw, we done tore the house up. Everybody hair is all wild. My clothes, buttons all tore off, shoes scratched. I had blood dripping off my head where she hit me with the hammer.

Police open the door. Man, I was so *glad* to see them muthafuckas.

I said, "Come on in! Come on in—'cause she trying to start some shit!"

Bernie Mac and Dick Gregory.

She hollering, "Oh, I ain't started nothing yet!"

They said, "What's wrong, Ma'am?"

She said, "He here, he firing on me."

I said, "She hit me, too! She hit me, too!"

They said, "You want to press charges?"

She said, "Yep!"

I say, "I'm pressing charges, too!

We *all* going to jail! Boots, get your clothes on! You going with us! We ain't gon' have no babysitter! We all going to jail tonight.

My wife was like, "You got-damned right! And we gon' finish what we started when we get there!"

We didn't have a whole lot of fights like that, but we had our share. I tell that story because it's true. People think because you married you can't have differences and stuff like that. That's not true. That don't mean y'all don't dig each other. That don't mean y'all don't like each other, man. It mean y'all human. You got to go to point A to get to Z. Now we don't do that no more. But before? Whew!

And during that one there? For some reason, that sister was possessed. That sumbitch fought me like I did something to her sister or something. I called her Thor for a long time.

Some women like to cut ya. My wife, she ain't never cut me— but she always talked about it.

You always know when they going for a knife. When they cussing—and that drawer open? When you hear that drawer with all those jingles? That's when you start, "Hey, hey, man. *Hey, hey!*"

They always open it—but they don't never bring it out. They just want to let you know.

They open it and then they talk to you: "You think I'm bullshitting? Keep on fucking with me. Keep on!"

You like, "Ain't nobody bothering you, woman. Ain't nobody bothering you, ain't nobody bothering you."

"I'm, I'm, I'm just—I done told you!"

And then they close the drawer back up.

But she ain't never cut me.

But yeah, me and Rhonda, we humbugged. I was Ali, she was Frazier. When I was bobbing and weaving, that muthafucka was rushing. She was rushing and cussing, "C'mon, muthafucka, let's box! C'mon muthafucka, why won't you stand still?"

I was weaving like Ali. I was moving.

She screamin' at me: "C'mon, you acting like a little bitch!"

I'm like, "It's all right, muh'fucka. The name of the game is 'I-hit-you, you-don't-hit-me.' "

Now, some people might try to say, "Oh, Bernie Mac, you promotin' domestic abuse."

Bullshit. That ain't domestic abuse. And if you say it is, you's a lie. I ain't promoting no domestic abuse. I'm telling you what happened in my life. Now, if you want to hide what happened to you in your life, that's your right.

But I guarantee you, you done had some discrepancies with your wife. You been with her for X amount of years, she done threw some blows. Yes, she has. You ain't always been the man that you are right now. I know I wasn't. I'm a much better man than I ever was. Right now, today? I appreciate it. I know what's in front of me. I see what I've gotten. I appreciate what I got. I took for granted, and that's the worst thing you can do is take for granted. The love I have for my wife. Man, I reflect back, and I couldn't have the love if I didn't have those fights. I couldn't have the love that I have if I didn't have those trials and tribulations.

I really wouldn't know how much I appreciate her, if she wouldn't have came at me like Joe Frazier.

And she kept coming, too. One time, I gave her a right hook—*bam!*

I swear I heard a voice in my head: "Down goes Frazier! Down goes Frazier!"

Man, I stood up over her ass, man, and the nigga came out in me. "Now! Now! Now!"

She got on one knee. All of sudden I heard somebody say, "He's up! He's up!"

She got ah eight-count.

Now, I look back, and I say, "I wouldn't trade Rhonda for nothing in the world, man!" I wouldn't give a care, can't nobody come and take her place, man! She refused to let me disrespect her. She refused to let me dishonor her. She refused to let me treat her less than what she was. So for people reading this, you take from it what you want.

But it's the truth.

And you have had it, too. Your woman done scratched you or something. You done shook the shit out of her or pushed her. You done 'bowed her in her titty or something. *Got-damnit, I done told you! Quit playing, muthafucka!*

Y'all done been in the car, and your car done zigzagged. She done scratched the shit out of you while you're driving. "Aw! Ohh!" Sweat done got in the cut. "Oh! Go on! Go on!" "Oh, hell naw!"

And there go the kids, "Y'all stop it, y'all stop it!"

A woman will whoop your ass. You'll fight a man. But it's just something about that woman. You'll be like, "Man, cool that shit out."

Because she can take a punch. You seen a man and woman fight, that shit be a *humbug*. Man be backpedaling.

MAN: She bit me all in the side!

You just hear someone going, *"Argh, arrr-gnaw."*
"Ahhhh!"

I 'bowed the shit out of that muthafucka. I had to get her off of me.

I'll tell you about another time we got into it. It was over my daughter and a party I told her she couldn't have.

See, I've always thought I was a decent father, but as I grew and my daughter grew, I'd say I was a great father. And I'm not saying that for credit. And the reason I say I was a great father is not because I stayed like I was supposed to—but I was constantly there. My daughter and I were in communication with one another at all times. She never was distant from me. She came to me for advice, and I gave her guidance. I told my daughter the truth, and a lot of times she thought what I was sayin' was real cold.

Sometimes, I would tell her no for no reason—other than to teach her I said no for no reason. Just to let her know that "no" exists because my daughter had the best of everything, from my in-laws, from my family, from me and Rhonda. My daughter had a birthday party every day of her life.

And so for her sweet 16 she asked me if she could have a party. I said, "No."

It might have been cold. Why did I pick her 16th birthday? Because it meant more to her. And I wanted to let her know to get ready for disappointment. You had birthday parties when you were one year old, two, three, four. So on her 16th birthday, I said, "No."

And the muthafucka threw a party anyway!

I was out of town. Went on the road, came back that Sunday. And how they got busted was a phone call.

It was a big thing about this party. I kept saying, "Everybody knew how I felt about the party." So I was gone on the weekend. I came back and the phone rang, and they was sleep. I had a few of my buddies over. We drinking beer and everything, chilling. And I said, "Hello?"

He said, "How you doing, Mr. Mac."

I said, "I'm doing good."

The voice sounded just like my cousin Greg, so I said, "What's up, Greg?"

He said, "Naw, this is such-and-such."

I said, "Yeah, hey, man."

"I left my speakers to my stereo. I wanted to know when I can pick 'em up."

"Man, Greg, quit playing! I'm tired and shit."

He said, "This is not Greg, Mr. Mac."

I thought it was my cousin Greg busting my balls about Boots not being able to have a party. I said, "Greg, I'm not bullshitting man, quit playing."

He said, "Man, I'm not playing."

So I hung up. Dude called back. He said, "Please, Mr. Mac, don't hang up on me. My name is such-and-such, and I deejayed for your daughter's party."

I said, "My daughter ain't had no party here."

He said, "Sir, yes she did. I deejayed."

I said, "Look here, I ain't gon' tell you no muthafucking more, man, a'ight?"

Man, I went in there and woke Rhonda up. I said, "Some dude called here talking about he deejayed, left his speakers and shit down there. Y'all had a party?"

A minute later, all you heard was, "They fightin', they fightin'! *Ahhhh! Ahhhh!*

"Down goes Frazier!"

My daughter was a great girl, though. I never really had to get on her about too much. I can count on one hand how many times I had to whoop Boots.

And one of them whoopings started up one of them humbugs between me and my wife.

My daughter was outside. It was kinda late, and she knew to

come in at a certain time. We had company over, my cousin and her boyfriend. And it was getting kinda late. I said, "Where's my daughter at?" So I went outside and walked to where she was supposed to be playing.

I walked, and she was nowhere to be around.

I went around the corner, I went on the next corner. I walked up and down the alley. I can't find my daughter.

Finally, I'm walking down the alley, and this car pulled up. My daughter get out of the car. It was a lady driving: "Uh, she went to the mall with us. Don't be mad at her."

I said, "Get out of that car! Get out that damned car right now!" Man, I took her upstairs. Before I did, the lady in the car was saying, "Mr. Mac, it was my fault."

I said, "Ma'am, you ain't got nothing to do with this. She know better." I told my daughter, "You don't go nowhere without telling me. I don't even know this lady!"

Man, I took my belt, we was upstairs. I was so mad. Man, I whipped her. I hit her on her butt; she was hollering. I say, "Don't you ever!"

Rhonda said, "Don't hit her again, that's enough!"

I hit her again.

She said, "Got-damnit, don't hit her again! I told you."

I said—*pow!*— "I told *you!*"

Down goes Frazier!

Man, they had to come betwix us. I think she was trying to get that same bite. She knew that spot was still tender from four years ago.

It wasn't just the humbugs. It was some arguin' goin' on. I'm coming in late. Rhonda mad 'cause she think I'm spendin' too much time with my boys.

She like, "You out there running the street with your niggas— and we sitting up here about to get put out!"

"Look here, look here! You just get the fuck out my face!"

"Why don't you put me out your face, Bernie! Put me out your damn face, Bernie!"

My wife's sister: "They getting ready to fight! They getting ready to fight."

"You better get your damned sister!"

"I'm sick of him! I'm sick of him! I'm sick of that muthafucka!"

"I'm sick of you, too!"

"You gon' come home, Bernie, and I'm gonna be gone!"

"Go! Go! Sick of your ass, too! Fat ass."

"Ya *mama* fat!"

I'm pointin' at her: "Hey, hey, *hey*! My mama dead, now! My mama dead!"

"Good!" She ain't got nothing good to say: "Ya mama dead! Good!"

No matter what we went through, though, I was in love with Rhonda from the beginning. I was crazy about her. We fell apart at times—but the love was always there.

If you get married for the wrong reasons, it's not going to last. We had personality clashes: she was growing; *we* was growing. I see a lot of cats who didn't make it, and they didn't put in the effort and didn't really love that person deeply. You look at marriages now and there ain't no such thing.

I talk about the fights we had. With some couples, the first fight and they're gone. They don't fight for love. They don't fight for their girl. I fought for mine. And that's a big difference. Their marriages, man, the first time they had an out, they took it. That's why their marriages don't last but eight months, or two years, and then they gone.

Like I tell my daughter, who's getting married: "Damn love. Love has its place. But y'all got to like each other."

If y'all don't like each other, love ain't gon' handle it. You can fall out of love real quick. Let that refrigerator be empty. Let that electricity keep going off. Let that landlord put a five-day notice on that door and see how much your love can stand.

Get laid off or don't make the money you want to make. See how long that love lasts. She ain't got no clothes, she got one dress and those same shoes she wore on prom. Okay? See how long that love last.

But like each other and you can stand everything that comes along.

Me and my wife struggled with money early on. I mean, we was broke. Man, I was so po', I tried to get my wife to steal money out of the cash register at her job. You know you low when you tryin' to drag your wife into shit with you.

I was on the phone with her. I was like, "Can you get 'bout $25 out the register? Try it. Try it."

I was po', man. I got off the phone and said to myself, "That's a damn shame, man. That's a damn shame. Call her back."

That night, I prayed: "Lord, help a brother out, Lord. Father, I'm askin' you for your help."

Back in the day, brothers who used to have a lot of women used to call them all baby. They'd call 'em all "baby" because they couldn't remember their names.

"Come here, baby." "Where you going, baby?"

That's when you couldn't remember because you had about six, seven women. 'Cause you was slick.

Her name was Tina, but you called her Grace. "Got-damn it, Grace. I mean—"

"Grace?"

"Man, I said—c'mon, naw—I said, 'This is *great*.'"

"You ain't say not muthafucking 'great'! You said—you said—you called me Grace!"

So back then, brothers used to say "baby." Because you can't go wrong, You can't go wrong if you call a woman "baby." "Look good, baby." "You hungry, baby?" "Where you going, baby?" "Hand that to me, baby." You can't go wrong.

Rhonda told me, "Call me *Rhonda*. I'm sick of that 'baby' shit."

She's the one pulled my coat. " 'Baby' is for when you got a lot of bitches and you ain't sure who you're with."

I'm all flustered, like, "Hey, hey, *hey*! What you mean by that, now?"

One time Rhonda asked me, she say "Have you ever committed adultery?"

I said, "Huh?"

"Have . . . you . . . ever . . . committed *adultery?*"

I said, "You?" You got to flip it around, ask 'em, "You?"

"You tell me your'n, I'll tell you mine!"

"Naaaaaawww, I ain't never . . . And if I did, I wouldn't say it."

That sum'bitch is scared. I got to go to my grave with that information. I got to go to my grave!

Bernie with Byron Woods and the Moods.

I don't care what you *say*. What's important to me is what you *know*. If you don't put your hands on me, it ain't me. Everybody got somebody *look* like them.

It ain't me. Whoever said they dealt with me during my success is a *lie!*

When I first shot the pilot to my TV show, I came home from LA and played it in front of my family and friends. Butter, Big Nigga, my in-laws—the people who had been with me while I was struggling. I just wanted to share it with them, get their thoughts and ideas on it.

Everybody liked it and everythang, man, but there's this one scene where I kiss my TV wife. Man, Rhonda ain't like that shit.

Now, everytime she sees that part, she be lookin' dead at me. Like, *mmm-hmm, muh'fucka.*

I be lookin' straight ahead. Ain't sayin' nothin'. I play like I'm busy. She say somethin', I go, "Huh?"

She like, "Yeah, I don't see you kissin' *me* like that. Ya look like you was enjoyin' it."

(*Sigh.*) Man, niggas won't let you be professional. See, black folks ain't used to being actors. Those ain't jobs to us. That's a luxury. They don't look at it as work.

They think 'cause I'm laying on a woman, open-mouth kissin' her—I'm between her legs grindin'—they think we serious. The shit's actin'! But they don't look at it like that.

OK, so your dick might be a lil' "heavy."

> **MOVIE DIRECTOR:** Cut! Great job, guys. Uh, Bernie, you
> was kinda *hard* in that scene.
> **ME:** Just doin' mah job.

I wasn't "strong." Just a lil' "heavy."

But I do my own stunts, man. If I'm gon' to sit up there and go through the glass door, I gotta go. If I gotta kiss the woman, I'm kissin' her. I gotta do what I gotta do. I told it to my wife.

So now, I can't sit around when we get to that part of the pilot. It ain't nothin' but a peck on the cheek, but so what. Everytime we get to that lil' part, I gots to get up and go get drinks.

That part come on, I just jump up and am like, "So, uh, anybody need more brews? Some water? Some milk? How 'bout you?"

It don't work. I come back, she just following me with her eyes. *Mmm-hmm, muh'fucka.*

Now, we ain't got nothin' but four love scenes in the TV show. I told my wife that when we do it, she cannot be on the set. She needs to be at home. I'm serious. Rhonda will mess everything up!

The shit'll be all in *Jet*: "Rhonda Mac went *off!*"

She come to the set, she gon' be tryin' to compare: "He don't do me like that. He pumpin' *for real!*"

My wife is a nurse. I don't go to her job and give medicine to the patients, like, "Here, let me help you, baby." I don't be doin' charts or takin' nobody temperature. So stay the hell outta my business!

I done laid down the law! I'm serious! Fuck around, we'll be on *Judge Judy!*

It's my first chance at television, and I ain't gon' let nobody take it away from me.

I'm pretending, okay? I'm pretending like I'm fuckin' her, but I'm just pretending!

That's why I haven't done any love scenes in my movies. I stay away from that. Rhonda likes to fight. A love scene'll bring the nigga out. I don't feel like bein' up all night arguing.

See, TV is restricted. Kiss here, then they cut.

Movies, your booty be showin'. I can't show no booty? And be twistin' it, too? Nah.

I know whoever the girl is, she go home and her man be arguing.

ACTRESS: What's wrong with you?

BOYFRIEND: You fucked him, didn't you?

I try to stay away from that. That's trouble.

Unless you makin' love to an ol' obese muh'fucka. Your woman can't see you fuckin' somebody 350 pounds, so they know you actin' then. They'll forgive you.

But let it be some Halle Berry or Jennifer Lopez or somethin'.

Man, that's them hippity critters.

I ain't got no outside woman, I ain't got no outside kids. I ain't got no vices with drugs, alcohol, cigarettes, stuff like that. Matter of fact I'm clean. All I need is some sandals, a robe, and a stick, and I'd walk on Lake Michigan.

My wife, she runs my company. Been knowing her since she was 15, I was 16. We tight.

But got-dammit, I can't do *nothing*. My wife gotta know *everythang*.

My assistant is in on it, too. I have my little office downtown that used to be my sanctuary.

My assistant messed that up: "Your wife wants a key."

My wife asked me. I said, "What you want a key to my office for? *My* office?"

She said, "Well, in case I want to show it off and show some people."

"What you doing showing people *my* office? This is where I work, where I come down and try to create."

She gon' go behind me and ask my assistant. She gon' put the squeeze play on her: "Uh, you know, I want you to get me a key made."

Then my assistant gon' go, "Well, uh, Bernie, Rhonda wants a key."

I said, "She talked to me about it already. Don't worry about it. Let me handle it. Don't you worry about."

Three days later, Rhonda come lettin' herself in.

My assistant gon' tell me, "Oh, by the way, Rhonda said she wanted a key and I got one made. I forgot that you told me . . ."

Now you know that ain't nothing but some old low-down bull-shit!

Work for me and gonna *betray* me! I ain't never forgave her for that! Ain't nothing but a ol' stool pigeon. I ain't never forgave her—and me and her man tight as a pair of draws. But that's one thang, man, she was supposed show her loyalty.

Women, they're the 12 Faces of Fu Manchu. You can't trust 'em, man, you know what I mean? They're in the same union.

No matter what you do, women, they're insecure. If I come home late, man, my wife put her hands on me. If my wife call me and I take 15 minutes to call her back? Muthafucka got a problem. That's my fault. I did that: because everytime she call me, I call her right away.

A half an hour, 15 minutes? You know she can't just say, "Hi." She got to know where I am. "Where ya' at?"

Damn.

It ain't that I don't know the answer to the damn question. But man, I'm a grown ass man. I gotta feel like a little boy again.

Mama'll say, "Where you going?"

"I'm going down the street."

"Where?"

"Around the corner."

"Which corner?"

"Right there, the blue house."

"Which blue house? It's four of 'em."

That's how my *mother* used to do me.

Man, I'm 43, and I feel like I'm a little ass boy. You know, "What you eat today?" She just called and asked me what I want for dinner—and now I got to go home like it's eight o'clock. The street lights come on, I got to be there. If I ain't there at eight

o'clock, this muthafucka mad. See, I did that. I spoiled all of
them.

My daughter's in with 'em on that type of shit, too.

I can't say somethin' bad without her gettin' on me. "Daddy,
you ought to be ashamed of yourself."

They always hear you say wrong shit when you they daddy. But
when it comes to they mama? All of sudden, she deaf. Mama can be
cussin', yellin' and shit, but she don't know nothin'.

> **ME:** You hear *that?*
> **DAUGHTER:** Huh?

One reason my wife and I only had one child is we were dealing
with our careers. My wife's a nurse, and I was doing comedy. So
after Boots, there would have been so much of a difference in age,
we said, "Why?"

I didn't want to be 44 and my baby's five, four. Because I wanted
to do the same thing I did with my daughter. And that is grow up
with her. And at the time, being young, my wife wasn't really keen
on having another baby. She wanted to get her life together. And I
respected that.

Do I have any regrets? I have some. Kinda sort of wish I had another one. Then I think on the flip side: Would the other be just as
great as the first one? Because my daughter is great. My daughter
never gave me any problem. She's an excellent daughter and person.

And just my damned luck: I'd have another one and the muthafucka'd be a criminal. Stress me out. Go to the lineup and got to
pick him out.

My wife got bad seeds on her side of the family. We were lucky
on this one. I just know; I just feel it in my *bones,* man. That
sum'bitch ain't gon' be no good. I ain't never told Rhonda, but I
know that muh'fucka ain't gon' be no good. I ain't gon' lie to you.

I don't want no hoodlums. Her family got some hoodlums. We doing too much good. She doing good. I'm doing good. My daughter doing good. The devil, man, he gon' throw a wrench.

Probably my grandkids gon' come around and be messed up. You got to have one.

Look at the Smith family that lived on my block. They had eight boys and girls.

Every last *one* of them was criminals. The girls was hoes, and the boys was gang-bangin' thieves.

And the mama, man, was about 6' 8" with no teeth on the right side. They say she used to play with the Globe Trotters. If you said that shit, her kids would tear your ass up.

Still, people used to call her Meadowlark Lemon.

With my daughter, I never had those problems. I never had to worry about her fallin' in with the wrong type of people or nothing. I mean, she coulda brought home a homeboy.

She got that thump in her. I'm glad, too. I want her to have that nigga in her. So she can take her earrings off—or the new thang now, takin' out ya contacts—and get ready to serve a motherfucka.

She handles herself like a lady, but she'll bring out the nigga. One time, I was watchin' her get ready to fight. I was standin' by just to let her know I was there. She's very soft-spoken. But that time, I heard "muh'fucka!" Her voice got a lil' deep. I said, "Is she a man?"

A girl was talkin' 'bout she wanted to fight my daughter. My baby was just like, "You better hope somebody around so they can break it up."

She brought out that nigga.

I'm very happy with my daughter and how she's turned out. She's going to get her master's degree. She's doing wonderfully for herself. I have no complaints. She never gave us no real trouble, and she was a great young girl. Now, she's grown up into a beautiful young woman who's about to get married.

The guy she picked is a good guy, too. He sincerely likes her, and he has character, style, ambition, and desire. I respect the young brother.

They have my blessing and won't have any interference from me—as long as there is no physical stuff, we cool.

Now, if there is, there'll be another book. And the title'll be some shit like: *How Did You Kill Him?* Or *Where's The Body?* Or *What Gun Did You Use?*

They'll have a picture of me on the cover of the book with a stocking cap on, with a title like: *Where Did He Go Wrong? What Made Him Snap? What Gun Did You Use?*

I'll be sitting up there doin' interviews butt-naked on a couch in the jail.

I was cool with everything about my daughter, but when she started havin' sex, man, I had a real hard time with that. I ain't gon' lie. When she hooked up with her first boyfriend, that was trial and tribulation for me. By her being my daughter—and me being the hypocrite I am . . .

You *are* a hypocrite in that situation: You want pussy, but don't want nobody messin' with your daughter. Man wants all the pussy—but when it come to *his* daughter, he wish he could sew it up.

When she told me she was "seein' " the guy, my heart was like, "Damn."

My daughter was a good girl, very mature for her age. So the trust thing had always been there.

When I found out she was involved with the cat, man, a friend had to talk to me for a *while*. I was so hurt and crushed, man. I ain't know how to handle it. It was hard for me to deal with it.

It got to the point where I ain't even speak to her. We started speaking again after she got inducted into the National Honor Society. She was sitting on the stage, and I came up to her nonchalantly and said, "Congratulations, baby girl." I kissed her cheek, and she started crying.

I finally realized how wrong I was. I told her I was sorry.

But it was hard, man.

You know how men are. I'm with my nephew, I'll be spittin' venom all day. When we got boys, we tell them to protect themselves, "put somethin' on ya strap."

Then when you with your girls, it's "Keep ya legs closed! Don't give a nigga nothin'! Take a aspirin, it'll go away!"

Seriously, man. You can come in and catch your son doing it, and you don't say shit.

> DAD: Junior, hurry up now. You know better than to be fuckin' on my couch. Bust a nut and send that girl on home.

But a girl? Your daughter? You come home and catch a girl, man, you'll grab the middle of ya chest. You be 'bout to cry.

> DAD: You just like yo' mama, no good motherfucker! Just like yo' grandmama and yo' mama! That's where you get it from—her side o' the family! All of 'em hoes! All of 'em!

Men want *all* the pussy. It's, "Look at the ass on *that* muhfucka." "Nice titties on her." "She got a mouth, boy, ooo."

But you got a daughter? "Keep your eyes to yourself, nigga!"

I was at the gas station, and I met a guy who said he used to go with my daughter. This nigga talkin' 'bout some damn sixth grade. What he really was tryin' to say was that he used to be with my

With Tia and Tamara Lowry of Sister, Sister.

daughter, but he ain't say it like that. "Yeah, me and yo' daughter, we was close."

I got the gas pump in my hand, right? I said, "Man, if you don't get away from my damn car, nigga, I'll make you a damn match."

You'll be hearin' about the shit on the news: "Bernie Mac burnt the shit out a motherfucker at Shell gas station!"

NEWS REPORTER: What happened, Bernie?
ME: Man, the muh'fucka came talkin' 'bout being with my daughter. So I made him a human match.

* * *

But as hurt as I was about my daughter having sex, I had to be fair. I thought about it. I met her mama when I was 16. We was kissin' and huggin' and the whole nine yards.

I'm a hypocrite. I used to go over her mama house and play with her mama while her grandmama was on the couch sleeping or at work. Come in and the whole living room smell like ass. I was tearin' Rhonda ass up every time I got a chance. In a car, at a beach, in a closet. In a stove. In a refrigerator. We almost smothered to death. Ol' Winehead came along and opened it up and saved our lives.

So the experience of dealing with my daughter maturing in that way, that experience made me a better person. I matured. I knew it couldn't be just what I wanted. I realized there are a lot of hipitty critters walkin' 'round this sum'bitch.

I messed up and learned to stop being a hypocrite.

I don't know how to raise a perfect child. Ain't nobody got a manual on that shit, man. My daughter has told me how many times I hurt her and I ain't even know it. She asked me one time, "Why you so hard on me?" I told her that's tough love.

I ain't got no spare, baby girl. You are the only child I have.

I'm not gon' apologize for being a father. But I learned that I can deal with her from another perspective.

Stop being a hypocrite, man.

Face it. You'll show your son how to hit it. You will teach him how to get some pussy. "Move ya hip like this, man. Yeah, they like when ya hit it like that."

If I had two or three kids, I don't know how I would be. I see a lot of instance where parents have kids and you heard kids saying, "I never got away with what he got away with."

You raise two or three kids, and the last one gets away with murder.

By me having one, I wanted too much. I had big expectations for my daughter—and she's meet them and then some, man. But I had to learn how to back off.

Sometimes, I put too much pressure on her. I could have really messed her up. By me being so cold and strict, she might've been a damn lesbian.

But my daughter always had nice taste in men. She ain't pick no poot-butts. They were always good guys.

But you know, I still had to make sure and let the niggas know.

I'd be all nice, invite the nigga to do shit. Man, I took one of them niggas huntin' with me, right? Let the gun go off by his feet. You know.

Blam!

"You all right, nigga?"

I got the gun pointed at him and shit, smiling and talkin'. I tell him: "Man, many accidents happen huntin'."

So now she's about to get married, and I think that's great. He's a nice guy who has his head on straight. And he's getting a good woman.

My daughter wasn't one of those girls with a bunch of dudes in her life. As far as I know, she was only with those two guys.

Now she's living away from home with her fiancé. And I know they play house where they live. And there's nothing I can do about that. That's on them.

But when they come to my house? Oh, no. Ain't none of that goin' on. They can't stay here together. Come in and it's ooohs, and ahhhs and shit? Oh, no.

Ain't nothin' but one dingaling in my house.

You go to your mama house. Get a hotel. But I ain't got *that* open-minded yet. I'm not going to sit in the next room and listen to you with my daugher. Sorry, it ain't g'wains on.

Tell you a true story: They came home for Christmas one year, my daughter and her fiancé. And when they came, it was during a snowstorm.

This was only the second time we had met him. It was snowing when they came in. We helped them bring in their stuff. My daughter unpacked. We all talkin', right?

So my daughter gon' tell me, "Daddy, it's snowing outside. Can he stay over? I know you ain't gon' make him go all the way to his mama's house in this weather!"

Now grant you, it wasn't snow—it was a blizzard.

I ain't give a fuck. I wanted him out.

Rhonda told him he could stay. I ain't care if he had tennis rackets on his feet. I wanted that nigga *out*.

I told him he could spend the night this time. "But he ain't spending the night tomorrow!"

He's over in the guest room. I went in there and slept with that muh'fucka.

Somethin' else that got me. While they were home for the holidays, I noticed that my daughter was picking him up, dropping him off. Running back and forth to take him around.

Now, I'm from the old school. I used to ride the bus to go see her mother. I rode the bus winter, spring, summer, fall. Rhonda's father never dropped me off. I don't give a fuck if it was below zero out that muh'fucka. When it was time to go, I got my ass on the bus.

And he did right. You ain't fuckin' my daughter *and* I'm droppin' you off. You ain't gettin' livery service.

So one night, it's about 12 midnight. My daughter gotta drop him off. She leaves, and she calls me back about five, six in the morning. She talkin' about, "I fell asleep. We got here late, and I didn't want to drive back in bad weather."

I said, "Who you think you bullshittin'? He should have jumped his ass out the car while it was still movin'. Nigga shoulda tucked his knees and rolled."

So the next day, I saw him and I says to him, "Come here, let me talk to you, man."

I told him I didn't want her dropping him off somewhere. I told him, "You a man. Think about it. She's out on the road by herself. If something happens to her, you ain't gon' do nothin' for her. You'll be too far away. My daugher ain't got no business leaving the house at one, two in the morning droppin' your ass off."

Man, the nigga got tight with me, man. He ain't speak to me for a couple of days.

I ain't give a fuck.

So New Year's Eve comes. We all over to the house, my daughter, my wife, him, me. I had my shotgun. I went out back, fired it off.

Blam! Blam! I came back.

He lookin' away.

I looked right at him: "Happy New Year's, muh'fucka."

I asked him if he was tight. He told me he ain't like what I said to him, that I came on him wrong.

I said, "Let me tell you somethin', *partner*. I don't care about you being mad. I told you the truth. I don't want my daughter being played for a sucker. You a man; I expect you to treat her like you're one."

He eventually understood where I was coming from, and he got over it.

But shit, I don't care if he didn't.

But yeah, like I said, I know they down there playin' house where they live. I call down there, it's 12 o'clock. I said, "Where's Trey?"

She says, "He right here. He just visitin'."

Yeah, right, muh'fucka. Nigga ain't just visitin'. That nigga up in there in his draws sittin' around watchin' TV. He live there!

I can accept that. That's what they do down there.
But in my house: Oh, no.

Every man wants a woman pure.
But we like a ho. Somebody on the side. Somebody nasty. Somebody who'll swallow it all.

> ME: Man, fuckin' will kill ya nowadays. Shit, I ain't too keen on fuckin'. Pussy ain't nothin' but hard work. All that pumpin', man. Man, I used to make love for an hour and a half. Until it hurt. I'd be chafed. Just raw. She just be layin' there: "Do you feel it?" You just be dry fuckin' after a while. Just burnt up. You gotta put some petroleum jelly on that motherfucka.
>
> One time, it was so raw, I had to put some Crisco oil on it 'cause she ain't have no Vaseline. It was burnt up.
>
> Now? I ain't lookin' for no fuckin' like that, man. You get yours. I get mine. Three minutes. Let's get this shit over wit'. It don't take all night.
>
> FRIEND: Aw, naw, man. You gotta go longer than three minutes.
>
> ME: How long you go, man? Four or five? Aw, c'mon, man.
>
> FRIEND: I'm more adventurous, man.
>
> ME: I ain't talkin' about the fo' play and all that bullshit. I'm talkin' about pure-dee fuckin'. You ain't gettin' nothing but about 90 pumps. 'Bout 90 pumps.
>
> FRIEND: *Pure-dee* fuckin'? Aw, I'd say I can go 'bout seven . . . seven, eight minutes. I want to make it last, man.
>
> ME: See, that's what I'm talkin' 'bout, man! Seven, eight minutes is a *looong* time, man. That's about 130 pumps!
>
> FRIEND: I pump slow, man.
>
> ME: All right then, I'll give you a hunnit-thirty-five. Eight

minutes is 'bout 150 pumps, man. I'll give you 150
pumps, but that's 'bout it.

FRIEND: See, that's you. We're different.

ME: Okay. How many pumps eight minutes give you?
How many pumps you get in, man?

FRIEND: I *don't know,* man.

ME: How many?

FRIEND: I don't count pumps, man.

ME: Gimme an estimate, man.

FRIEND: I don't count pumps, man. All I know is—

ME: Naw, c'mon. Count the pumps, man.

FRIEND: Since I've been working out . . .

ME: We ain't talking 'bout since you been workin' out!
Count ya pumps, man. How many pumps you get off,
man?

FRIEND: I . . . don't . . . know, man.

ME: Approximately. You're a mathematician.

FRIEND: I don't know, man. It depends on what I'm
doing. I gots to see. It might be *300* pumps.

ME: A'ight, a'ight. Once you slide it in. Once you slide the
hog in, right? *Pow!* That's one pump. *Pow! Pow! Pow!*

FRIEND: Ain't nobody talkin' . . .

ME: Naw, naw. Hear me out, man. A'ight, you still
pumpin' . . . *Pow! Pow! Pow! Pow!* That's eight pumps . . .
Pow! Pow! Pow! Now you goin' at angle, at 45 degrees . . .
Pow! Pow! Pow! Pow! Then it's, *"Agggggrrrhhh . . .
ohhhh . . . awwwwwwwww."* That's 25 pumps, man!

FRIEND: Naawww, man. You gotta get up, get her to turn
around.

ME: Bullshit! Naw, man, that's bullshit! I count 25 pumps,
man. You get up and turn her around and she pull that
ass to you, you can't even look at it! 'Cause if you
look at it, you're gonna explode! If she got a full moon

and she turn around, you holdin' that shoulder, you can't look at it going in and out of there. *Ugghhhh, ewwwwwww,* you gon' bust.

FRIEND: Naw. You don't look at it.

ME: All right, you look at it and what happens?

FRIEND: Oh, you look at it, oh . . . it's over. Especially one of them asses with the tuck. You stick a pencil between that thigh and that booty and it stay, that mean she got a tuck. She move that motherfucka it'll be over. You call them "ceiling booties." You gotta look at the ceiling when you hittin' that ass.

ME: I hate when they twirl that ass. That drive me bonkers. I can't be around no shit like that. But see, niggas lie on they dicks, man.

FRIEND: Naw, naw, man.

ME: Unh-unh. Niggas lie. Lemme tell ya something. I been black a long time, man. Niggas lie on they dick. "Man, I was in that motherfuckin' pussy, I tore that shit up all night. I fucked three times, then I rolled over."

FRIEND: Aw, I ain't sayin' that. But I used to.

ME: When you was 21, 22, yeah, we did do that. But we ain't doin' that shit now. You don't do it. You a damn lie!

FRIEND: Used to be, you go to a hotel for eight hours, you might get 20 minutes sleep. You'd fuck for four hours.

ME: Yeah. Your mattress be tilted. Box springs all fucked up.

FRIEND: But now, you go for eight motherfuckin' hours. You figure you gon' fuck about 12 minutes.

ME: Shit, he *givin'* hisself an extra four minutes.

FRIEND: And then you gon' sleep about four hours, and rest of the time you watchin' TV.

ME: Sho' is. And you gon' get up and eat 'cause you went and got some ribs and some chicken. And then you don't want to see no mo' pussy.

People always ask me about the kids who I talked about when I did that "Milk and Cookies" bit in *The Kings of Comedy*. The kids actually done turned out all right.

When I first got them, man, they was ignorant. They better—but that's training. They was ghetto-ized. They couldn't complete a whole sentence. Just ignorant. You know how you get a dog and he ain't trained and he chewing on the couch and all? That was these suckas. They was chewing on the couch. Piss all around the toilet—wouldn't even wipe it off. You come you sit on it, and you got a wet ass. Just nasty, you know.

So now, they're obedient. The oldest girl, she doing good. She got married, got two kids. She married a guy in the Marines, made a career.

The little one, she's growing up, she's doing real good. She's a good student, and she's gon' be going to college.

It took training, man. It took love. But it was hard. They used to stress me the hell out. That was the first time I was under some *stress*. I was getting the older girl's hair done every week. I had the little one in school. Man, she was taking the little girl out of school, gang-banging. Smoking reefer in front of her. It was a transition.

The boy is doing great, too. My nephew is very, very smart, on top of his game.

But he still a faggot.

He just know he is now. He didn't know then. Now, when he walk past a man with a big booty, he hums.

Hmmmhmmmm.

That's a fag there. A homosex'yal. But he gon' be what he is. I still love him.

Chapter Six

In Case I Didn't Mention

Recently, it was hot outside. Hot than a muh'fucka. 100 degrees. Devil smilin' and shit. The sun is *hot*. I'm too dark, man. Naw, I ain't shamed to say it: I'm too muh'fuckin' black. When I looked in the mirror, I said, "You's a black motherfucka, boy." I started to come outside butt-motherfuckin'-naked. I got some shoes to match. They sharp than a motherfucker.

Black women don't cook when it's hot either.

> **HUSBAND:** Why don't you cook me somethin'?
> **WIFE:** I ain't cookin' a motherfuckin' thang.

You wanna get on your woman's nerves? Just say, "Damn, baby, you kinda stank."

"You a motherfuckin' lie! That's your top lip, motherfucka!"

If you tell black people they stank—black people're too clean, man! We don't like nobody talking about you musty or somethin' like that, man.

Just fuck wit' ya woman. When she come by and try to hug you, you know, just say, "Damn, baby, what the fuck you been doin'?"

"What you mean, what the fuck I been doin'?"

"You kinda tart. Kinda tart."

"Yo' mama tart! Yo' mama tart!"

Now she wanna talk about my mama and shit, see.

Black women somethin' else. I love me some black women, boy. But black women, they want to be your mama, your father, your woman, your pastor. They want to tell you what the fuck to do all the got-damn time.

You go out to eat, they wanna order for ya.

GIRLFRIEND: Naw, he don't need nothin' but a salad.

Don't order for me! Don't order for me! I'm hungry than a motherfucka right now. Salad my ass!

BARTENDER: You want a drink?

GIRLFRIEND: No, he don't need nothin'. He had two beers already.

ME: Bitch, I wanna get drunk tonight! Don't fuck with me!

What type of shit is this?

You can't drive. You be drivin' all nice and smooth, going to pick your woman up, man. You be singin' with the radio and all that type of shit.

Soon as you pull the fuck up and she come out the door, there it go, it's out the motherfuckin' window. Here she come, gettin' on your fuckin' nerves: "Slow down. Watch that light. You see those kids playin' over there? How come you ain't park there? Back it up!"

Shut the fuck up talkin' to me! Before I choke the shit out you! Shut up!

Bernie Mac and wife Rhonda McCullough.

I love you. But black women gotta run shit. Black women always wanna tell you what the fuck you can't do. Especially when it's company around.

GIRLFRIEND: Uh, no, no, no, no, no, no, *noooo!*

What the fuck you mean, "Uh, no, no, no, no, no, no, *NOOOO?*" I'm a grown motherfuckin' man.

And if you get a page? Man, I don't give a fuck where you are, if you with your woman and somebody page ya? You better call somebody the fuck up. You better call *somebody* back, I'm not bull-shittin'.

> **VOICE ON PHONE:** Hello, police department . . .
> **ME:** Is John in?
> **VOICE:** Police . . .
> **ME:** John!

'Cause she lookin' at you. Hard, too. That's when they take a long "blink."

And if you don't call?

> **GIRLFRIEND:** Ain't you gon' call?
> **ME:** I'll call him later.
> **GIRLFRIEND:** Why you can't call him now?
> **ME:** 'Cause I don't want to, mammyfucka, I don't want to!
>   Nosy sonofnabitch!

You know I ain't lyin'. Black women somethin' else, man.

See how the world is now? I'm gon' show you how the world changin'. Water used to be free. The shit is $2 now.

By the year 2000, if you ain't got your shit together, you gon' be fucked up. If you and your woman ain't tight, you gon' be fucked up.

See, everythin's changin'. Milk changed. I love me some milk. But I can't drink no motherfuckin' milk. I'm lactose intolerant. Milk fucks me up. If I drink some milk, you gon' have to get the fuck away from me. I'm tearin' that room up! *Fffffrrrrrtttttttttttt!*

You'll be like, "Gotdamn!"

You ever have a fart pain that come up by your heart? *Fffffrrrrrttttttttttt!*

You be like, "Man, that feels so much better! Got-damn!"

You ever have a fart and your covers shook? *Fffffrrrrrttttttt!*

Your woman be asleep; she just roll over, but she cuss you out: "You nasty motherfucka!"

How you sleep under that funk, man? I cut a fart the other day, and my wife was laying in the bed. I took the cover and put it over her head. All I seen was the bottom of the cover kickin' like a motherfucker!

All I heard was, "You tryin' to kill me!"

Everybody do it. Everybody.

But when you're with your woman, and she passes gas, she thinks it's cute.

Fffrrrrttt!

"Hee-hee-hee. You heard that?"

Like it's gon' be all right.

"Yeah, I heard it, you stankin' ass! What the fuck is wrong wit' you?"

A woman, on the first date, when you first meet her? And she cut a fart? It takes years to cut a fart in front of somebody, man. That means you tight. You got a relationship. You don't just meet a woman and she think she can just poot in front of you, like y'all "strong."

You take her out on the night, you bring her to the door. "You know, I really enjoyed myself."

"Me, too—" *Fffffffttttttttt.*

You be talkin' to yourself: I know this bitch ain't farted!

You know I ain't lyin'. All of us human. Everybody make mistakes. We're human.

Me and my wife been together a long time; we've had our humbugs. Oh, we've had our humbugs!

You ever had a humbug wit' your woman, and y'all ain't speak for two weeks? Oh, that's some distressed shit! See, I'd rather cuss and fuss and for you to throw somethin' at me. But you don't talk to me for two weeks?

I don't know what's on you mind. I can't go to sleep around that kind of atmosphere. You ain't sayin' shit to me but want me to lay down. Everytime that motherfucka got up, I got up, too.

You read the paper: Motherfuckers'll fuck you up, man.

You ever had that thing with your wife where she's coming down the hallway? You're coming from one way, she's coming from the other. Y'all don't wanna touch and shit. Y'all *sliiiide* by and shit.

And black women, they're a trip. When they're mad at you like that and don't want to talk to you for two weeks, and the phone rings? They won't let you know. They'll just pick up the phone.

Riiiingggg.

WIFE: Hello? Hold on one minute . . .

Then they just put it down on the table and walk away.

Two hours go by.

WIFE: You get the phone?

Hell, naw, I ain't get no got-damn telephone!

Or if you got kids, they say, "Go tell your daddy, 'telephone.' "

You ever run your kid when you and your woman was fussin'?

WIFE: Tell ya daddy to come eat!

CHILD: Daddy, she said come eat.

HUSBAND: I don't wanna eat!

CHILD: He said he don't wanna eat.

WIFE: Tell him that's all right with me!

CHILD: She said that's all right with her.

HUSBAND: Tell her I don't give a fuck!

CHILD: He said he don't give a fuck.

Two weeks go by, man, and see, the power of the coochie is a bitch. Women got the power 'cause they got that ol' pink eye. Coochie is something else. Coochie been in power since B.C. And it's been fuckin' motherfuckers up. All those Egyptians lost they mind over a piece of pussy.

Pussy can kill you and go to court and get off. Because women start that fuckin' cryin' and shit.

> **WOMAN:** (*Sob . . . Sob . . . Sob . . .*)
> **JUDGE:** Take your time.
> **WOMAN:** (*Sob . . . Sob . . .*)

Let you, a man, get on the stand and start some fuckin' cryin'. The judge'll cuss your ass out.

> **JUDGE:** What's the problem?
> **MAN:** Boo-hoo . . . Boo-hoo-hoo . . .
> **JUDGE:** Answer the question, motherfucker! Answer the
>   question!

Two weeks go by, you ain't had no pussy, you know you hot. You wanna make up. But as man, you can't do it. It's not right! Any man who make up first is a punk.

Hold out! Fight it out! I know your dick hard. I know you want some. You *shakin'*. She ain't helpin' none—she walkin' around with some ol' raggedy panties on with a big-ass hole near the crotch.

You sittin' in the chair, your dick so hard it's leakin'. But you don't want to say nothin'. She know what's up. Big-ass hole. Coochie just sittin' out there, just sittin' out there.

She come bendin' over near you, askin' you a fucked-up question while you all hard: "You seen the TV Guide? Huh? Oh, here it is. O-oh, I dropped it. Here it is."

You lookin', lookin'.

Now, she walk out the room, stay for five minutes. Come back, ol' raggedy bra on, one titty all out, just hangin' out, nipple stickin' out like a .22 bullet. She scratchin' it and shit. Oh, you really hot now!

Then she go in the bedroom. Now you got to go in the room behind her. 'Cause you gotta play like you lookin' for something. You ain't got shit you lookin' for. She standin' by the dresser, you gon' walk behind her real close.

> HUSBAND: You seen . . . Uh . . . You seen my watch?
> WIFE: Get off me!
> HUSBAND: Ain't nobody on you! Ain't nobody on you!
> WIFE: You are on me! Get off me!
> HUSBAND: Ain't nobody on you!
> WIFE: Get off me, motherfucker! Get off me!

Now, y'all wrestlin'. You throw her on the bed, breathin' hard, tryin' to get your knee between her legs so you can pry it open.

> HUSBAND: Open yo' motherfuckin' legs! Stankin' ass!
> WIFE: I'm not givin' you shit!

Now, you finally get in there. You kissin' on her. She movin' her head left and right.

> WIFE: Uh-unh. No, no . . . you . . . no—

She finally start kissin' you. Now, y'all both fuckin' and screamin'. Then, you know you done bust a nut 'cause you start gruntin'. Need about ten pumps!

> WIFE: Aw, you motherfucker, you done came!

Now, she done came. Both of all y'all breathin' hard, like, "Whew, Shit." Y'all lookin' at each other. Here come the bullshit . . .

> **WIFE:** Bernie, Why you do me like that?
> **HUSBAND:** You did me like that.

Punk ass!

See, I respect women. With a man, you get into it, you can tear some furniture up. With a woman, you hit her, she'll go in that kitchen and open that drawer up and start messin' with them knives.

You hear that silverware jinglin'; that drawer open, and she start screamin' "I'll kill ya!"

Get the fuck on outta there! She start cussin' you out with her eyes closed—"Motherfucker, I done told your motherfuckin' ass!" Get the fuck on outta there!

When you go get the gun and don't know how to put the bullets in that motherfucker? Get the fuck on outta there!

When she go in the garage and get that axe and come back swingin' that motherfucker backwards? Get the fuck on outta there!

When she get up and break the glass and hold a piece in her hand while she's bleedin' like a motherfucker? *Get the fuck on outta there!*

A woman will kill you, man. A woman will fuck you *up*!

My wife a lil' short motherfucker and always wanna argue all the time: "What? What?"

Short motherfuckers always wanna argue with somebody. "Who? Who?" Lil' Miss Shortsum'bitch wanna argue with me. Lookin' up at somebody.

*   *   *

My wife like to argue on bullshit. She think I ain't goin' nowhere. She think she gon' be with me forever. She's complacent. I just might flip out and do a brother move on her motherfuckin' ass. You know, how a brother get a lil' money and just go. Get a white woman or somethin'. I might act like I forgot to get gas the other day. She gon' blow a motherfuckin' gasket.

> WIFE: You get the gas?
> ME: Damn! Fuck! That's what I forgot!
> WIFE: No, don't get nothin'. Don't get a motherfuckin' thang.
> ME: I'll go back and get—
> WIFE: I said don't get a motherfuckin' *thaaaaang!*
> ME: What the fuck you singin' for?
> WIFE: Because I want to motherfuck*aaaa!*

They'll just make up a song on your ass.

> WIFE: Black ass motherfuck*aaaaaaaaaaa!*

I'm lookin' at this crazy-ass sum'bitch.

> WIFE: You act like you wanna hit me?
> ME: Now, why would I want to do that?
> WIFE: Because you starin' at me.

They think because you're staring, it's gotta be related to wantin' to hit her. But I'm just lookin'.

> ME: Ain't nobody said nothin' about hittin'.
> WIFE: Well, I just wanna know—'cause I'm here! I'm here!

What the fuck that mean, "cause I'm here?" Now, I done got caught all up in the shit.

ME: Well, I'm here, too!

WIFE: I'm here.

ME: I'm right here! I ain't movin' no motherfuckin' where, either!

I accidentally slapped my wife the other day. I ain't gon' lie to you. She kept fuckin' with me. I told her to go on. I told her!

She kept fuckin' with me and aggravatin' me. She "marked" me: Everytime I'd say somethin', she'd say it.

I said, "Quit playin'!"

She said, "You quit playin'!"

"All right!"

"All right!"

"I done told you!"

"I done told *you*."

"You think I'm playin'?"

"You think *I'm* playin'?"

"Say somethin' else!"

"Somethin' else."

Kept fuckin' with me. So I tagged her. I must've enjoyed it 'cause I hopped. In the back of my mind, I'm screamin', *"Beee-yatch!"*

She left, didn't come back for nine hours. Now, I'm callin' all over the place tryin' to find her. I called my mother-in-law's house. She knew what happened 'cause she was short.

ME: Hey, Ma—

MOTHER-IN-LAW: Hi.

ME: Rhonda over th—

MOTHER-IN-LAW: Noshe'snothere.

ME: When you see her—

MOTHER-IN-LAW: I'lltellheryoucalled.

I hung up. *Fuck you, too!*

*   *   *

Black funerals? Don't go to no more black funerals. Bar 'em. Because black funerals are full of shit. I'm serious. They make me sick. Layin' up there in the fuckin' coffin for three days, and we gotta go see this motherfucker, and he dead for three days. What the fuck we gotta go sit down and watch this motherfucker in the coffin for three days for?

White folks, you die tonight they bury your ass tomorrow. I like that about them. They have a funeral for 45 minutes and the lights on. It's bright. Bright curtains and everything. The guy sings, *Oh, Lord I'm so happy God saved me!* And then they close the fuckin' coffin. If you ain't see him, you fucked up.

Us? Three fuckin' days. He die, we gotta take some clothes over there, like he goin' some-motherfuckin'-where.

And something about black people: When somebody dies, black people love to find out how you died.

OLD WOMAN 1: How he die?

OLD WOMAN 2: Girl, I was rollin' my hair and I heard a thump. I went downstairs, that motherfucker was on the floor dead. I knew somethin' was wrong 'cause it was rainin' and I was rollin' my hair. I heard a thump. I had to put my gown on. And I walked downstairs, and he was layin' against the stove. I didn't get a chance to finish rollin' my hair, 'cause I heard that noise. He was layin' there! (*Sob . . . sob . . .*)*Layin' there. I knew somethin' was wrong 'cause I was rollin' my hair! And I heard a thump! And I walked downstairs! (Sob . . . sob . . .)* ain't have my house shoes, neither! And this motherfucker was dead.

Boy, the doorbell rang, and I never will forget! It was a Friday! And I was rollin' my hair! And I heard a thump! I walked down there, my brother was layin' on the floor dead! Oh, God, he was dead! I said, "Oh, Lord,

Bernie Mac and daughter Je'Niece at his surprise birthday party.

I gotta call my sister and tell her!" 'Cause I heard a thump! I knew that motherfucka was dead!

Then you got the wake. Why they call it the wake? He ain't wakin' up! You gotta sit there and watch this motherfucka in the coffin! Every now and then it look like he breathin'.

And she down at the end of a bench, "I was rollin' my hair."

Shut the fuck up down there!

And then black preachers . . . I'm sick of 'em. Why black preachers can't just come out and say, "For God so loved the world that he gave his only begotten Son. Yes, he did. And whosever believes in Him shall not perish, but shall have everlasting life."

Why they can't just say that shit? It's gotta be dramatics, theater. Why the preacher gotta growl at us?

> **BLACK PREACHER:** Heh-heh-heh . . . I-I-I . . . I just wanna
> tell *somebodeee* . . . Heh-heh. Okay? I just wanna *tee-ell*
> *somebodeee* . . . Aw, whoa, Lord. Oh, Lord! Hunh-hunh!
> *Ohhh, Looordd* . . . I just wanna tell somebodeee . . . Tell
> it! Tell it!
> **OLD WOMAN 2:** I was rollin' my hair.

SHUT THE FUCK UP!

Then after they do all that, they gotta introduce some fat woman to come sing some song. Now, don't nobody know this heifer. The funeral parlor people don't know her. The deceased's family don't know her. Ain't nobody asked this heifer to sing.

She wanna make you cry—on purpose. She gon' sing an ol' song, "Precious Lord." But she gon' rewrite the shit. So here she come with her fat ass . . .

> **FAT LADY:** First, givin' honor to God, the pastor, mem-
> bers, and friends. I'm so happy to be here this evening,
> by the grace of God. Hallelujah! Hallelujah! Hallelujah!
> I want you all to bear with me as I attempt to sing this
> song, "Precious Lord Take My Hand."

This how she wanna make you cry. She clears her throat.

When I want to get in tune, I go back into the city. That's what got me here, that kind of humor. We don't know what we have until we don't have it anymore. We lose perspective on what life is really about. Money, success—all that's fine. But everybody ain't living like that. They don't have the mentality. They're still under the struggle. Still living check to check. Something get broke, they gotta prioritize. We had to prioritize. You need gym shoes for gym, but your auntie need glasses. I think we better go with these glasses before she go blind.

You miss those days. Do I want to go back? Hell, naw. But I can't forget either.

I have an agenda. My office is downtown, right in the middle of the city. When I go, I let it flow. I'm spontaneous. That's where my humor and my life comes from. I don't know what I'm gon' do. I don't know. That's when I have the most fun, when it's not scripted. When I go to the city and I see something, I put it on tape. That's how I write. I let it come to me. I don't come to it.

I just got news today that my man Art Porter—he died not long after doing Midnight Mac; his boat tipped over and he drowned—I just found out his wife died in January. Now his kids are orphans. I asked my assistant to find more information on them. I want to see if there's anything I can do. I like doing stuff like that.

I don't like to be told where to give. I don't like to be told what I need to do for the community. I like to give for many different reasons. I don't give for superficial reasons. Because it sounds good or because I want to be commended on something. I do it because I believe in that donation. I believe it's going to benefit the people.

I was listening to Whoopie Goldberg. Brother asked if she gave back to the projects she come from. She said no. Audience went "Ooooo!" Whoopie said, I don't give a damn.

I left 69th in 1971. I don't know nobody from over there. And I got a tribe of nieces and nephews who need my help. That's my community. I ain't been criticized. I don't have to make an announcement. It ain't nobody's business where I give. That doesn't bother me.

I give where I want to give. You worry about where you give and what you give, those who want to will criticize.

I used to sponsor summer programs. Wasn't making much money. It was $70 a kid for the summer. My wife looking at me like I was crazy. I had to "help the children," you know. But we sittin' over here hungry as hell.

I was doing 12-hour days, opening and closing. Dealing with the kids. Swimming, basketball, football. And I enjoyed it. Because it gave me joy. When I saw those kids, I saw me.

I think it's unfair. First of all, it's none of your business. That should be your main focus, on yourself. It's not your business to tell Oprah Winfrey what to do. Some people are politically endowed to do stuff like that.

Bill Cosby done helped a lot of people. He done sent a lot of people to school. All those things are great. Richard Pryor has helped so many people. Redd Foxx was a giver. It's their business to give to whom they want to. People critize for numerous reasons: they're envious; they want something and they want to bash you.

I'm lookin' at *Real TV* recently, and I'm lookin at these bulls tearing these cats tails up. White folks crazy. White folks crazy. They be messing with wildlife. I saw a lion caught in some trap. This cat gon' go release the lion from some trap. That lion ate his butt up. Ate everything, his clothes and everything. He ain't got no business messin' with the lion.

White man, he sees a bear in a tent, he go over there with some fruit. The bear thought *he* was the apple.

You better leave well enough alone. I was watchin' one show where this deer was laying down. He was sick. Guy went over there to where the deer was. Man, the deer was on two legs fightin' this guy. He was kickin'. Those hooves was knockin' hair off his head.

White folks better leave these things alone. They always meddling. If I see any kind of wildlife, *maaan* . . .

There was a fox in my shed one time. Rhonda said, "There's a fox who done made himself a home."

I'm not going back there. I'm not messin' with no wildlife. That's why they say "wildlife." That mean they ain't tame. They ain't got no sense. A lot of animals have nervous breakdowns, man. They'll tear yo' ass up.

People see a cub in the woods and they want to go and mess with it. "Oh, look at the cub!" But they don't be thinkin' that if that cub is there, that mama is not somewhere far off. All that cub gotta do is whistle. That mama'll come kill you.

Then people want to take up a collection for somebody who died like that. "Um, he died last week. A lion killed him in the forest."

I'm not givin' nothin'! He ain't have no business meddling. Leave things alone.

He'll see a racoon laying in the street and wanna go help him. But he ain't dead yet! Leave him alone.

I told you about me and rats. We used to have rats everywhere. They scared me. Somebody'd say, "A rat's by the refrigerator." I'm like, "Look, as long as he ain't by us, don't bother him!" Leave that rat alone. That rat'll crawl up your legs. *Whooooo* . . . your skin be pink. I don't mess with nothing like that.

Black folks are conservative. They ain't jumpin' off no cliff. We ain't bungee jumping. Ain't too many of us skiing—unless they went to Stanford or some shit like that.

I'm lookin' at these cats on these skateboards. You don't see too many black kids doing that. Flipping, riding down banisters, hurtin' theyself.

See, we don't like no pain. Black people, we gotta look sweet. You playin' baseball, you swinging and everything, missin'. You struck out everytime. Zero for four. But you looked good!

We shootin' basketball, done missed the whole rim. But your *form* was *perfect!*

A brother boxing, he's shuffling, bobbing—and ain't hit shit. But he's sweet! His shorts match his shoes. His hair's combed. He looks like he's goin' to a barbecue.

The people out here catchin' on fire doing dumb shit. I wouldn't throw no water on 'em. I'd let three-quarters of their bodies get burnt up.

Bungee jumping. Why you want to jump off a cliff and *almost* hit the ground? You're a 16th of an inch from the ground, and you're like, *"Whooo!* I almost bust my head *wide* open! *Whooo!"*

This guy was out on his boat one day. The people were telling him there were twenty-foot waves out there. They told him don't go out to sea. But he's going *yachtin'.*

Man, that boat flipped over like it wasn't nothing. He in the ocean screaming. Ain't no need in hollering now. The Coast Guard goin' out there. If I was them, I'd take my time.

People in Miami having hurricane parties, celebrating possible death. "We might get swept out! Yay!"

I like simple things. I like swimming in shallow water. I like to swim where I can stand up in case I get tired.

Something's I just ain't doin'. You ain't shootin' me out no cannon. Something might go wrong. Or that shit like playing with wild animals on TV, like Johnny Carson used to do? I ain't doin' that shit.

I was watching a TV program not too long ago, and a woman was interviewing a bear trainer. Now, the bear was sitting up there next to the woman, with a muzzle on his mouth. I guess the woman thought the bear wasn't gon' do nothin'. So the reporter playin' with the bear and shit.

Man, Yogi tore her ass up. He clawed the fuck out her ass, man. She come sitting next to him like he stuffed. The bear said to himself, "Oh, she don't think I'm real." He looked at her twice, like, "I'm givin' you a chance to break off and run."

She stood her ass right there. He tore her *up*.

I don't play with animals. The TV people on my show were like, "Bernie, we're gonna have a mongoose on the show and—"

Uh-unh. Nope. We ain't havin' shit like that.

They had a *Leave It To Beaver* marathon on one day, and I was watching. They had this episode where there was a gopher in the backyard. Ward gon' set a trap. Man, that gopher ain't nothin' but a big-ass rat! I ain't messin' with that. He can eat what he wanna eat back there.

Growing up, I had a dog named Bullet. But he just wasn't right.

He used to stay out late and come in when he wanted to. He got one dog pregnant down the street, but he wouldn't take care of his kids. I'd leave the door open. Rhonda'd be worried about him.

Then he got sick on me. He caught diabetes. He lost a lot of weight. But he kept on drinkin'. Hard-headed, man. He sellin' drugs. We had to put him to sleep.

It might have been the food. He wasn't eatin' no Gainsburger. He ate what we ate: ham hocks, collard greens, macaroni and cheese, cornbread, chicken. He got high-blood pressure. His hair started fallin' off him. He had an ulcer.

And when he got the dog pregnant down the street, we was all surprised 'cause he was gay. All he used to mess with was male dogs. He'd be sniffin' 'em, tryin' to hum. We used to have to throw hot water on them to break them up.

We tried to mate him with another full-blooded German shepherd, but he fought her all night. But he finally got him some. I think he was high, though.

My grandfather gave him away. He was from the South. He ain't believe in keeping those dogs.

* * *

Bullet would tear something off. He wasn't no chump. He could jump off the roof. He'd jump off, and the kids would go running. A few minutes later, they'd come ringing the doorbell: "Bullet loose." The roof was 20 feet high. He jump off. He'd come back, ring the bell, act like nothin' happening.

I didn't have a favorite comedian coming up, but I had admiration for so many. I had a love for comedy, for what comedy brought and what it did for people. It didn't matter to me. Funny was funny. Black, white, male, female.

Carol Burnett was funny to me. Redd Foxx, Richard Pryor. I thought Red Skelton was great when he got into character. Jackie Gleason was hilarious to me. What he did was naturally funny. He never rehearsed. They say he was drunk half the damn time. You can't give nobody that.

And Moms Mabley, who I really was a fan of—influenced me. I took a page out of each and every one of their notebooks. Stu Gilliam. I liked Jack Benny. His facial expressions and his body language. His timing was impeccable. He ain't say nothing, but he was funny as heck.

Harpo Marx made you laugh without saying a word. You come out and the audience laughin', and it just be his body language.

Flip Wilson was a great comedian. Bill Cosby was a conservative comedian to me. He dealt in the era when everybody was red, white, blue, and apple pie. He did his part. He represented in a positive way. Richard Pryor was funny. He made you laugh at yourself. He made you feel like it was a part of you. He didn't come at you as a celebrity.

Redd Foxx came in when everything was politically correct. Redd Foxx been doing it. Look at Lucille Ball. Tim Conway.

The Three Stooges was funny. I'd have killed Moe, though. I'd have taken him out in his sleep. Slapping you with a hammer upside the head, cutting Curly's neck with a saw. He took something hot out the oven and when Curly was bending over, put it on his back. Moe would been dead messing with me. He was slapping people for no reason. He'd slap Larry and hair would be flyin' every-where.

Curly'd be looking at him like, *I'm sick of this muh'fucka!*

He'd just tell Curly, "Scram!" Moe was abusive. Moe had prob-lems, man. Moe ain't love nobody. He was cheap with money. He'd be counting out his money: "One hundred . . . two hundred . . . three hundred . . ." Then he'd give you a quarter.

He was cheap with bread. He was supposed to share, but he would just give Larry the butt of the bread. Yeah, Moe woulda been dead messing with me.

I watched the high school cats get drafted. I'm waitin' for the first grammar school cat. He's gon' be 9'4", 467 lbs., and he'll stut-ter. They gon' draft him anyway: "You can't stop him from making a livelihood." You offering a cat $21 million, and he ain't passed his SAT test, what he gon' do?

The guy the Bulls got, Eddy Curry, he's playin' in his home-town. Now, that's pressure. He's 18. By the time he gets 21, he's gon' be sick of everybody.

Family gon' bother him.

> **AUNTIE CURRY:** Baby, give your auntie 20 tickets. You know she never been to a ball game in her life. You know she old, on a respirator. She said, "The last thing I want to do is see him play."

All his boys from kindergarten gon' sweat him like hell.

His daddy done quit. He told his foreman, "Fuck you!"

> **FOREMAN:** You comin' in today?
> **MR. CURRY:** Kiss my ass!

Chaka Kahn and Bernie on the Midnight Mac Show.

He ain't go to work that day. When they drafted his son, he was like, "Aw, shit!"

You see the family on the side at the draft; they jumpin' more than the dude getting drafted. All of 'em quittin' they jobs. Baby cousin quittin' his job. Cousin on his daddy side, he quittin'. He works at the grocery store, talkin' about, "Fuck you! I quit! I ain't baggin' shit!"

Then, if Eddy Curry break his leg, they gon' kill him.

"Nigga got the nerve to break his leg!"

Or "Ain't but 21 and his back done gave out! 21! He's 6'7", 290 pounds—and hurt! Boy, I tell you."

Watch! He's gon' be sick of it. Relatives are gon' call his house—and he can't act like he ain't home. They gon' come over unannounced.

*   *   *

You see how the family be jumping, hollering? They ain't even all blood relatives. You see the lady you *call* "mama" 'cause you go over her house and kick it with her son. She jumpin'. She like, "Are you ready?"

"For what?"

"Ready to be drafted. You gon' go 1 or 2. They lookin' for big men now. You know what? I saw me this big car . . ."

The NBA goes through a transition. The guards take over for a couple of years. Then power forwards. Now, Shaq O'Neal has brought a new dimension to the center position. He kills people. He killed Mutumbo in the playoffs. Elbows all in Mutumbo's throat. You see in the newspaper pictures, everytime Shaq went up, Mutumbo had a different face.

I think it's gon' take about five years before you see anything from these new players, but the whole league is young. Karl Malone is the only one of the old cats. He looks like he on some kinda respirator 'cause he keeps going and going and going.

And I tell you, outta all the fights you have seen, don't nobody mess with Malone. Don't nobody mess with that mountain-climbin' nigga. Malone gotta be 38, and he built like a building. And still be running, getting up and down the court like it ain't nothin'. They call time-out, Malone be sittin' on the sidelines like he's Marvin Hagler, ain't even breathin' heavy.

Remember Marvin? He was in such great shape, you never saw him breathing hard. He would be sittin' in his corner and his people would be talkin' to him, and it'd look like he was dead. It was like he wasn't breathing at all. Then the bell would ring, he'd get up and go clobber the shit out ya.

You can't have sex with nobody like that. I know when Karl Malone comes home and ask for sex, it's a problem.

> KARL: Wanna have sex?
>
> KARL'S WIFE: Aw, shit. Damn. Well, I was *supposed* to go
>   over to my mother's.

You can't do nothin' with Malone.

Even Charles Oakley don't pick with Malone. And Oakley *likes* to fight. I remember the fight between Oakley and Xavier McDaniel, the X-Man. They was all in the stands humbuggin'. It was like they were fightin' over a broad. Now Oakley be beatin' up guys like Tyrone Hill.

Of course, Tyrone Hill looks like he been beat up already. He's not the most attractive man. If you saw Tyrone Hill in the grocery store, you gon' be like, *Somebody fucked him up!* "You all right, man?"

I ain't no Billy Dee Williams, but Tyrone Hill, he ain't a handsome man.

> AWARDS PRESENTER: And for the Ugliest Cat of the Year,
>   the nominees are . . . Sam Cassell . . . Tyrone Hill . . .
>   and Jimmy Walker. And the winner is . . . It's a tie!

They are tore off, man. Like cats used to say back in the day, "They ruint."

It's hard to find somebody who will stick with you, somebody you can have a foundation with. Rhonda been with me for a real long time . . .

I'm looking at her right now. Yeah, she been with me a long time. Uh-huh, she been with me a long time . . . a real *looooong* time . . .

Her middle name is Dinosaur, Cave Woman. She knocked me across the head with a bone, that's how long we been going together. She stuck by me when I ain't have no bank account. I had to go to the currency exchange to cash my checks. They take $6 out. My check wasn't nothin' but $66. I'd cash it, then we used to go Sizzler. You couldn't tell me nothing. A family outing!

They'd be waiting on me—her and my daughter—to take 'em to Red Lobster. That was before Red Lobster became a diner.

Now? I can't even drive past Sizzler or Red Lobster. It's, "I *know* you ain't goin' up in there!"

They want some five-star stuff now. See, I still had that lil' po' man mentality at first. "Let's go to Red Lobster."

Rhonda would blow a gasket: "We goin' over there where the salad is $48!"

Expensive, boy. Glass of water $25. You leave, the bill be $600. And you can't tell my wife nothin'. She be sittin' there, stomach full, lookin' around, suckin' on her teeth: "Aw, this is *beautiful*, *mmhmm*. Thank you, baby."

Then I got insurance. Aw, man, you shoulda heard Rhonda: "You mean if you die, I get $2 million? Aw, we doin' *good!*"

We used to get up: "I hope you don't die today." No medical insurance. No car insurance. I'd go to drive, Rhonda would tell me, "Be careful! You know we ain't got no insurance."

I'd be like, "I'm taking the side streets!"

See, there were rules to driving when you ain't have car insurance. On Fridays, you didn't drive from twelve to six. You had to let the traffic die down. Too many cars out.

Seven o'clock, it would slow down. You could go out after seven. But you had to be back in by eleven. 'Cause after that, people leavin' bars and drivin' drunk.

If somebody had hit us, they coulda took everything. They coulda took our *stereo!*

We had a nice stereo, the most expensive thing in the house. The couch wasn't worth nothin'. The loose spring in the cushion would stab you. We had books holdin' it up for legs.

We had that television with the black line going up and down on the screen. I used to have my daughter holding the antenna for three hours. "Just stand there!"

Her cousins would come over, and she would be glad. "You spendin' the night? Good! You can hold the antenna."

The kids would be like, "What?"

"You'll see."

Next thing you know, we got my nephew holdin' the antenna. His arm would get tired, we'd give him a Blow-Pop. He just standin' there, holdin' the antenna and suckin' on a Blow-Pop.

When we started moving up in the world, we got life insurance. Blue Cross/Blue Shield! Before that, we couldn't afford no medication. Anything wrong, we took aspirin.

"He got a fever."

"Give him some aspirin."

"He got chills."

"Give him some aspirin."

"He stepped on a nail."

"Crush up some aspirin and give it to him."

"He got a sore throat."

"Dissolve four aspirin in some water and gargle with it."

Rhonda said, "What if one of us would've died? We'd have been tore off."

But with insurance? Oh, man, people glad to see you go now.

"You mean to tell me, if you die I get $2 million? Keep on drinking. You got hypertension? Eat some more, eat some *moooore*."

We out eating one night, and my wife gon' say, "Yeah, we gon' be well taken care of if something happen to Bernie. Well taken care of."

I looked up from my food, like, *What the fuck is this? You plannin' somethin'?*

"Yeah, we gon' be well taken care of. Not that we *want* anything to happen—but if it did, we gon' be okay."

I had to keep my eye on her.

*   *   *

I got a guy who does wardrobe design for me, been dealing with him for years. One day recently, he brought my clothes by from the cleaners. He said my bill was $143. So I gave him an extra $100, then he left.

Right after he left, I'm lookin' at the bill, and I see where he done mixed his clothes in with my clothes. So I'm paying for his clothes and mine to be cleaned! And he ain't said nothin'. Done walked on out.

I found out later that it was a mistake that he didn't know about. But at the time, I was gon' get him for tryin' to 86 me, man.

You gotta set an example with people. I was thinkin', *He'll go out and tell people. They'll think I'm a lollipop.*

He's workin' on my TV show. I was plannin' to fire him before I found out it was an accident. I want people to be afraid of tryin' to do stuff to cheat me. I want 'em to be like, "Don't mess with Bernie. He'll fire you."

It wasn't gon' be over $243, either. Hell, naw. I was gon' make the deed small as hell. "Man, he took 75 cents and Bernie fired him!" "He took a beer out of Bernie's refrigerator and Bernie went *off!*" "Bernie had two watermelons in the refrigerator, and he cut one. Bernie *fired* that muh'fucka!" "He had on one of Bernie's belts and Bernie fired him. He was head of production! Yessir, Bernie don't be messin' around! He'll fire you for nothin'."

I'll just walk in, look at somebody: "You fired."

See, that's power. You know it's power when you fire somebody, and they ask for their job back. "Come on, Bernie, man. Bernie, can I talk to you?"

You fire him at eight o'clock in the morning and he still around at four o'clock in the evenin'. Oh, that's power.

I'm like, "You're fired! Security!"

He'll be waitin' for you out by your car. "Bernie? Bernie, can I talk to you?"

You get home, you're wife holdin' the phone, talkin' about, "Baby, phone call."

It's that cat: "Bernie? Bernie, can I talk to you?"

The white man done had that power for years. The black man, we coming along now!

See, black folks don't believe you're fired till you take the time card out the slot.

> FOREMAN: You're fired.
> BLACK EMPLOYEE: Yeah, right.

But take the time card out the slot?

> BLACK EMPLOYEE: Aw, come on, man!

He be bringin' up old personal shit.

> BLACK EMPLOYEE: We go fishin' together!

Brothers don't come to grips with nothing like that, especially if you fired him at the end of the shift. He gon' come in in the morning like ain't nothing wrong.

> FOREMAN: Don't punch in, man.
> EMPLOYEE: What?
> FOREMAN: Don't punch in. You're fired.
> BLACK EMPLOYEE: Man, you bullshittin'! You gon' fire
>   me 'cause I took my lunch early?
> FOREMAN: I told you, you're supposed to take your lunch
>   at three. You start at 11, you took your lunch at 12!

So I was gon' fire the guy. But first, I was gon' stop payment on the check I had written him for my cleaner bill.

That would've embarrassed the shit outta his ass 'cause he banks downtown where all the white folks at. You know you messed up when you go to cash a check, and they pull you to the side.

> **BANK CUSTOMER:** Uh, what's the problem, man?
> **BANK MANAGER:** You have no funds.
> **CUSTOMER:** Come on, man. That's bullshit!

People are lookin' at you, whispering: "He broke." It's embarrassing. I know. That happened to me.

I'm broke, right? So I wrote a check for $35, just hopin' I might be able to get it through. But I knew I ain't have no money.

But when I came to the bank, I couldn't let that show. So I walked through the line like I was *strong*, like I had a couple of thousands up in there. I handed the teller the check. I'm whistlin' and shit. A few minutes later, they're like, "Excuse me, sir, can we talk to you?"

I said, "What's the problem?"

I started to yell and stuff. Then the teller came over and said, "Look, you know you ain't got no money in here. Now just gon' head and go before they call security."

But you can't run outta there. You gotta walk strong, take long strides, so that in about three steps you at the door and the door is 50 feet away. Then you hit the door, and that's when you sprint out.

When white folks come to see you:

> **WHITE FAN:** I'm going to see Bern. Got-damnit, that's
> who I'm going to see!

Black people, we don't give a fuck about nobody:

> **BLACK FAN:** I'm going to see some nigga.

We don't give a fuck.

When you fart, ain't nothing worse than that mean, quiet muthafucka. That means that shit is close like a muthafucka. That's when you lock your ass.

You can piss on yourself and get away with it. But when you shit on yourself, muthafuckas bring that shit up ten years later: "Aw, shit, nigga. Remember when you shitted on yourself? Stanking ass bastard."

Ain't no fucking difference between black and white people. Stop that old bullshit. Quit saying everything the world tells you to say. Be your own person.

Farrakhan said, "Don't go to work," and your dumb ass stayed home. You know your lights gettin' ready to get cut the fuck off. Now when they put your ass out, call Farrakhan to come help you move.

White people, man, they don't care about how they look. They got their priorities together. They'll wear the same clothes. They don't give a fuck about how they look. They got their business together. We'll be clean than a sumbitch. And broke. Ain't going no got-damned where, but sharp! Nails done, hair done every day. You see this fucked-up hairdos our women be wearing around here? Chandeliers—high and hard. And when they get their hair done, you ain't getting no pussy. They don't even want no sleep. That shit'll be hard. Black women, when they get their hair done, that shit gotta last. They got it planned. They get their shit done on Thursday, no pussy on Friday or Saturday. You might get some pussy on Wednesday, when they need to get it done again. And you know how you can tell their hair needs doing? It starts itching. They be patting tha muthafucka. You know I ain't lying. Then they'll get a pencil and start scratching it. What type of shit is this?

We don't give no credit to nobody:

MAN 1: Jesse Jackson is over there.
BLACK MAN: Fuck Jesse!

Africans hate our asses. It's bad when you jet black with pink gums. That's ah ugly muthafucka there. And Arabs and shit—we sure be fucking with them. Go in the gas station: "Give me two cigarettes, muthafucka."

Black folks got a certain look on their face when they got to throw the fuck up. They swallow a lot. And when they get that look like they're smiling—they're about to throw the fuck up on your ass.

Black folks is a trip—come in to the show all late. Orange-ass hat too small. We got white folks in the house, and y'all coming in all late. That's why they be talking about us all the time.

WHITE WOMAN: Look at them, Joe. Fucking late niggers!

That silent muthafuckin' fart—you can start an argument with that. You and your boy can be as tight as a pair of draws. But let him *pssssssss!* and it get in your mouth: "Man, don't do that bullshit no more, muthafucka! Stanking-ass bitch! Trifling muthafucka!" You get mad as a two-year-old baby. I can't stand them silent muthafuckas. Grown-ass man smelling like pure-dee shit: "What's the matter, muthafucka, your water cut off?" My brother smells like shit. He don't even care; he just get all close to you smelling like dead-ass shit. You know, at first you think maybe they don't know they stank. They just used to it! Stanking-ass bastards! A musty muthafucka make me sick, too. He know his shit ain't working, but always want to talk with his hands.

We pay our bills when the fuck we're ready. And we ain't gon' pay all of it. The bill $125, we giving you $40. Because we got to smoke. We got to drink. If you don't drink or smoke, black folks think it's something wrong with you. Be on the job not saying nothing for three weeks, on the fourth week they coming at you.

> EMPLOYEE 1: So, hey, how you like it? You like it?
> EMPLOYEE 2: Yeah.
> EMPLOYEE 1: Where you be hanging out at? You smoke? You don't smoke? Nothing? You drank? You don't drank? You can't be trusted!

Know you ain't paid no bill, but you gon' argue. You be down at the light place and talking to everybody but who the fuck you're supposed to talk to. The lady right there (behind the counter), but you ain't gon' talk to her.

> BILL DODGER (to other people in line): Muthafucka gon' cut my muthafucking lights off! My kids and shit all up in there! What the fuck am I supposed to do now? I'll be done tore this muthafucka up!

Certain shit brothers just don't do. How you think they be solving murders and shit like that? Be twenty-something bodies up underneath a house. That ain't no nigga, that ain't no nigga. We too clean. Nigga can't stand a fart. Muthafucka leave a plate on the table and we got a problem. If you stank, we ain't going over your house:

RELATIVE 1: We're going over Debra's house.

RELATIVE 2: I ain't going over there. That bitch smell like sour pussy.

Oh, we'll tell it. We like to eat, but if you cooking and you nasty, we ain't eating shit.

White people be having papers all over their house and shit: "Come on in!" See, we nosy, first thing we do is we're looking around. Don't let us go in the wash room, we are going to open up your medicine cabinet. We're nosy, man!

We'll tell our business when it comes to paying bills.

BLACK PERSON (on phone with bill collector): I'm doing the best I can. I lost my leg in a car accident. It's just been me and my son. Lord know I ain't lying. Oh, Lord, Lord!

You can tell when a muthafucka is turned on: *"Ughhhhhhh!"* You ever been in a room full of grown folks watching a porno? I'll put the shit in on purpose—especially if it's old folks around. My auntie and them'll come over. I'll slide the thing in there, and they'll be trying to play like they ain't watching while they're trying to hold a conversation.

AUNT: Girl, I went over there and . . . and, when I saw that, yeah . . . Bernie what you done put on with your crazy ass? *Ughhhhh!*

Man, I fucked them old folks up. They about 55, 60. My auntie say, "You so nasty." Yeah, and you hotter than a muthafucka wasn't you. That grey squirrel poppin', ain't it!

* * *

Us, we're clean, sharp. Ain't going nowhere. Ain't no food in the refrigerator. Kids crying. But we look good. We got to look good—tight jeans, nails, hair all done—hey! That's some meaningful shit to us. White folks be like, "Why does that mean so much?" Because we ain't never had nothing! If you ain't never had nothing, you're always wanting. "Man, I wish I could get a job paying nine dollars an hour." That was some big shit to us. Nine dollars an hour? Get paid every week? Benefits? Boy, you was somebody. White folks always had good jobs. Man, we ain't never sit in no office. If we could just put on a suit going to work, we thought that was special. You thought you was somebody important. Smiling. That shit meant a lot to you. My point is don't be sad, don't be ashamed of who you are. I ain't ashamed of shit.

My first muthafucking suit I had was a three-piece suit. I wore the pants, my sister wore the vest, my brother wore the jacket. And was proud like a sumbitch.

> FAT LADY: Ahem. Y'all bear with me. I just got outta the hospital. *Pre-shus Lo-o-ord.* Ta-a-ake my . . . hand . . . Le-e-ead me on-n . . . Let me . . . s-s-s-sta-a-a-and . . .

She try to get you here.

> FAT LADY: Oooooooooooo . . . Oooo . . .

Bitch! If you don't put that microphone up! And while she's singing, she be lookin' at you.

Why you lookin' at me singin' like that? Like I'm next or something.

I'm sick of the bullshit. I'm over my brother's house the other day. My nephew came in the house. He's goin' to jail. He ain't got long, he ain't got long. He ain't no motherfuckin' good.

Bernie with Byron Woods and the Moods.

You know your kids. Quit bullshittin', playing like you don't know your kids. Just like Michael on *Good Times*. You knew he was a sissy!

We don't never say shit about no Chinese. But we sho' laugh at those muh'fuckas everytime we go to they restaurant. Don't you start laughing when they start with that *"Mong-mong-ming-dong-mang-mong"?* You love to hear their asses talkin'.

That's how they name their kids. They get a bunch of silver-ware, and they throw that shit up in the air. And when it hits the floor—pang-pong-ping-pang—that's what they name their kids.

You don't play with your asshole. I wish a muh'fucka would play with my asshole. What type of shit is this? I don't care how fine you is, you put your finger in my got-damn ass—pow!—I'll break your motherfuckin' jaw. Filthy bitch!

Fuck is wrong with you? You don't play with that asshole, man. You think I'm bullshittin'? When you put your finger in somebody's ass, watch the noises that come out that motherfucka!

You'll be like, "Hey! Hey! Hey!" My wife gon' rub her finger on my ass. I said, "Don't go up in there!" Don't put your hands in my got-damn ass. What type of shit is this?

> GIRLFRIEND: You mean so much to me.
> ME: Keep your fingers on the got-damn side!

The type of fart you cut tells what wrong with your got-damn stomach. If you cut one of those mean, heavy farts—*Rrrrrrrrttttt.*

> BYSTANDER: You just got gas. You just got gas.

When you cut one of those farts like it's tearing your slacks—*Flllrrrrrrrrrrfffrrrrttt*—you ate some bad ham or some shit like that.

Black folks like to keep up shit when we wrong like a sumhabitch. Black people the only people go to jobs and swear we run that motherfucka. I know white folks talk about our asses like a dog when they go home.

> WHITE EMPLOYEE: I'm so tired of these African-Americans, I swear to God.

We always keepin' up some shit on the job. Don't let it be no telephones in that muh'fucka. Shit, we gon' call everybody but who the fuck we supposed to call—and get an attitude when they tell us to get off the phone.

> SUPERVISOR: Hello, Bernie? I need you.
> ME: H-hold on, man . . . Got-damn, man, what is it?

SUPERVISOR: We need you over here.

ME: I'm comin'! Man, call me back in 15 minutes. This job
be trippin' like a motherfucka!

White folks do the same shit we do, they just do shit different.
They'll tell creditors to fuck off. "Fuck off!"

You know how creditors call you—like it's their got-damn money.

CREDITOR: When can you pay? Can you borrow it from
somebody?

Ain't that a bitch? Don't they?

CREDITOR: Well, how soon can you fuckin' get it, pal?

I told the motherfucker, "I got motherfuckin' money right got-
damn now! Come get it now, sum'bitch! I'm sittin' in the got-damn
front! Come get the motherfucker now!"

White folks'll tell 'em in a minute: "Fuck off! I don't have it! Ya
can't get blood from a turnip!"

Us? Bills scare the shit outta black people. When the creditors
call our house, we'll tell a lie on our got-damn self.

CREDITOR: Can I speak to Bernie?

ME: Uh, he ain't here!

CREDITOR: You know when he'll be back?

ME: Uh, he died this mornin'.

You know you're successful when white folks come to see your
ass. Then black folks come in and mess everything up. Show about
to start and white folks sitting their with their programs; they done
read the muthafucka and everything. White folks is cordial, they re-
spectful. Black folks come in late, their pagers going off.

That's all we hear: black this, white that. The white man this, the black man that. I'm sick of racism. The world ain't all black and white. White, black, Chinese—mixed—that's the way it's supposed to be. We all peoples. But all you hear is white this, black that. If I was Chinese, I'd be mad than a muthafucka: "They don't never say nothin' about me!" But we quick to talk about Chinese when we go to their restaurants: "Gimme a number fourteen, fifteen." Then they start talking that *"Beyong, yung, yeeng,"* and we kicking each other under the table laughing and shit.

Keep laughing at muthafuckas fixing your food. See what the fuck will happen to you. Chinese come back and feed your ass some cat or dog or some shit. You be barking all fucking night.

Man, don't fuck with your stomach. Your stomach is the most delicate thing on your body. That and your ass. When your stomach is fucked up, you ain't in no shape to do shit. When your stomach is fucked up, you know what you got to do. When you fart, your fart will tell you what you got to do. If you get a fart that go *brrrrr,* your stomach just hurting; that ain't shit. That ain't nothing but some gas. You cut that silent muthafucka, you get a fart that go *pssssss,* you got to shit. When you hear that *pssssss,* your ass is wet. Ain't nothing worse than a wet ass. Worst thang a person can do is fart and don't tell you. Especially if you getting ready to talk.

We all the same, ain't nobody different. I'm gon' tell it like it is. Ain't no difference between black and white. We the same fucking people, we all gon' die. White folks the same kind of people we are, we just do shit differently. Black folks, we the only ones go to our job and swear we run that muthafucka. I know white folks talk about us like a dog when they get home: "I'm so fucking tired of these Negroes, I swear."

Because black folks, you say the shit your got damned self when you get to the crib. "These brothers make me sick like a mutha-fucka." Don't let them go on break. White people go on break, you can find them. They sit at their desk and eat their sandwich and drink they fucking tea. When we go on break, that's just what the fuck we do—break. You got to look for those sumbitches.

And don't let it be no telephone on the job. We calling every-body but who we supposed to be calling. We gon' call our whole got damned family. And get mad when they tell us to get off the got damned phone. You'll wait for your supervisor outside.

You know they always talking about black folks are some violent people. Naw, we ain't. Black folks are some loving people. We just talk a lot of shit. We ain't gon' cut nobody up. We'll blow your head off. And cuss you out while we doing it: *Pow!* "Now, muthafucka!" White folks will chop your ass up: "Hold his legs, Joe!" We ain't gon' watch nobody get stabbed no 37 times. We can't handle it. After a few stabs, we're screaming: "You're killing that mutha-fucka! You're killing him!"

They say black people cuss too much. That's bullshit. White people can do some cussing too, now. Like can't nobody say cock-sucker like white people. That and asshole. You driving on the ex-pressway and cut them off? "Fucking cocksucker!" Everybody got their words. Mexicans got "punto." Blacks' word is muthafucka. We'll muthafucka you to death. Can't nobody say muthafucka like black people: mutha*fucka*. Look at how black people talk. (A muthafucka can be a person, place, or a thing.) You listen to a con-versation. You'll hear 15 muthafuckas. And one regular English word. But the sentence make sense like a muthafucka.

BLACK PERSON: Man, when I see that muthafucka, man!
   He owe me five muthafucking dollars. He ain't paid me
   my muthafucking money yet. The muthafucka told me
   he was gon' pay me last muthafucking Tuesday. I ain't

seen the muthafucka. But when I see that muthafucka, I'm gon' bust his muthafucking head!

You know I ain't lying.

Everybody say this group do this, that group do that. That's all bullshit. They say we fuck all the time. White folks fuck, too. They love to fuck. They on TV more than us, fucking. You see it on those x-rated tapes. (Our tapes be fuzzy and shit.) They just fuck for different reasons. White folks fuck for trust funds, insurance policies. They fuck for inheritance. We fuck for rent. Outfits. Light bills. We got to do what we got to do.

And everybody knows that when you get older, you're supposed to get better. I'll tell you for a fact, I ain't gon' lie. I'm old. I can't fuck like I used to. I'm not in shape. Sex ain't nothing but hard got-damned work, man. Ain't shit but some physical got-damned labor. Just pumping all got-damned night. What the fuck you trying to achieve? Fuck until your heart stop? Bullshit. Forty-five minutes, just fucking. Just fucking. Chest hurting, lips white. My back hurt, and she laying there talking about, "Right there! Ooh, right there!" What the fuck is a "right there"? Bust a nut so we can go to sleep. I'm tired of this shit. I'm old! She talking about, "I want to make it last."

"Bitch, you don't bust a nut, I'm gon' choke the fuck out of you. You ain't gon' kill me. I'm tired." You got your fucking clothes everywhere, mattress twisted and shit, pillows sprinkled every got-damned-where. And she sitting there going, "Cheee . . ."

Listen to the words that come out of people's mouth when they're making love. I be busting up because, see, I'm stupid. I'm not well. I be making love, and I'm listening to all those stupid-ass sounds. What the hell is a "Ba-ha-ha-huh"? I'm making love to my wife, and I did my thang and all of a sudden I hear, "Eh-hugh!"

What the fuck is "eh-hugh"? Bust a nut! All that hollering and groaning and shit, I'm tired!

I got a problem. I'm not ashamed to say it. I ain't putting on airs. I'm saying what you're scared to say because you think people ain't gon' like it when you tell the truth. I can't fuck no more. Three minutes. I'm weak. I went to the doctor, I say, "Doctor, something is wrong with me. I ain't the man I used to be!"

I used to be a sex champion. Man, when I got on pussy, I used to fuck the hair off it. Now I'm retired. My shit is on the wall of the hall of fame. I look at it and get mad now. My wife say, "You gon' come on and do something?" I try to find an excuse. "I'm going to Cleveland this week." Because I can't fuck no more. Three minutes, that's all I'm giving her. That's all I got.

My wife was playing with me in the bed the other day. We was in the bed naked, wrestling. I told her to hurry up. I told her to hurry up. I say, you know I ain't got long. You up here bullshitting. She want to wrestle and play. The next thing you know, I came all on her belly. She cussed my black ass out. I didn't give a fuck. I was asleep. I'm telling you the truth. Sex is hard work, man.

There's a time and place for everything. And women love oral sex. That's just the way it is. All you got to do is say, "Girl, I'll kiss your ass." Watch what she say: "When?" Don't even know what your name is.

Women don't like to have oral sex with me. I got a problem with that. Men been doing women for years. Ain't never complained. Every time you ask a woman to do you, they get an attitude, especially black women. You got to give clues: "Why don't you come over here and lay your head right here? Come here and relax." They'll cuss your ass out: "What the fuck you mean by that?" Share and share alike. If that's your woman, you got to give the best you got. Because if you don't you gon' lose her.

Don't be ashamed. Everybody needs love. I don't care if you're a preacher. Everybody needs a nut sometimes. In the name of the

Lord, you need it. Ain't no shame. But the messed up thing about that is kids.

See the world is messed up—kids. See, I'm saying what you're afraid to say. Kids make me sick. I can't stand those sumbitches. I'm not talking about the kids from the '70s, '60s, and early '80s. I'm talking about these '90s got-damned kids. Ooh, these sumbitches, man, I can't *stand* them! Ever since they changed the rules to stop you from hitting these fuckers, I lost interest in them. These some bad sumbitches. They ain't got respect for no damned body with they small asses. See, I grew up with Big Mama. Ain't no Big Mama no more. Ain't no more Grandmama. Your grandmama now, what—34? Great grandmama 34, grandmama 24. See, that's what I'm talking about.

I got a daughter in college. So the last few years of my life, me and my wife been living real swell. Nobody in the house but her and I. Then I got three new kids. What the fuck I need three new children for? Two, four, and six. These were my sister's kids. I ain't ashamed to tell you. My sister was on drugs. The state was gon' take the kids, you know. But I came in. Yeah, I said it, my sister is on drugs; I ain't ashamed. Some of your family is fucked up, too. I'm sitting in court, I should've sat there like my brother did. My brother ain't say a damned word. He just turned his got-damned head. When they said they were going to give the kids over to the state, he turned his head. I had to get my self-righteous ass up: "Naw, this ain't right. We're family. We got to stick together." If I'd known these bastards was like this, they'd be separated right now.

Man, when I got 'em, they was ages two, four, six! And that two-year-old, she was the sumbitch. That heifer been here before. She was an apostle for the devil, I tell ya! One day, I was combing her hair, looking for some numbers.

And the four-year-old, my sister musta really been getting high with her because she don't say nothing; she just look at you. I told her, "Heifer, if a fire break out, you better learn how to whistle or something. Or you gon' be a burnt-up bitch fucking with me." I ain't got time to be going into no fire looking for somebody like this. She just stare at you.

And the six-year-old cry like a sumbitch. But the two-year-old had control over the six-year-old's mind. Whatever the two-year-old would tell the six-year-old to do, he'd do it. He would run to do it. And she'd kick him, scratch him, beat him. And he'd cry like an old heifer all the time. He came in my room the one day, crying like a little bitch.

I knew what was wrong. I say, "Sabrina?"

He say, "Yeah."

I said, "Look in my drawer and gimme my pistol."

This heifer, she had to be stopped. She had to be stopped. She was bad.

I came home one morning, one o'clock in the morning. The two-year-old done sent the six-year-old down the stairs for some milk and cookies. He gon' walk past me like I'm a visitor.

I say, "Sir, where are you going?"

> **NEPHEW:** To get some milk and cookies.
> **ME:** Sir, it's kinda late. Go on back upstairs.
> **NEPHEW:** She wants some cookies now.
> **ME:** I don't give a fuck what she want! You better go on
> back upstairs before you get fucked up down here!

I don't mean no harm. That's how I talk to them. To hell with that time-out shit. I ain't got time.

He gon' go upstairs, and the two-year old gon' say, "Where is the cookies and shit?"

He gon' tell her, "Him downstairs."

Like I ain't got no damned name. Who the fuck is "Him"?

She gon' tell him, "I'll go get the shit myself."

She come waltzing down into the kitchen. Got a little step ladder, gon' open the refrigerator—and I'm watching. I said, "What are you getting ready to do?"

> **LITTLE NIECE:** Get some cookies.
> **ME:** Didn't you hear me tell your brother? You can't have no got-damned cookies. You open that refrigerator, I'm going to hit you in your doggone temple. I'm not bullshitting with you.

She gon' look at me like I stuttered or something! She gon' look at me up and down like I'm short. I said, "Get your ass upstairs!"

And they ain't never sleep. Up walking around the house at two, three o'clock in the morning. See, when my sister had these kids, she was on drugs. She must've been on coke and reefer. Because they're wide alert, and they're always hungry.

My wife and I couldn't even talk no more. I can't make decent love to my wife because these kids won't go to sleep. When you get older, your priorities change. And you got to change with it. I'm old, but when you got kids, you can't do the same things you used to do. We got to make plans to have sex.

These ain't nothing but words, but the truth is, these sumbitches made me sick! And if you touch them, they sue. What type of shit is this? I was going to be sued muthafucka, I tell you. Because I got me a bat and I planned on using it. They cut my love life out! And they weren't scared of nothing.

I was watching TV. Remember scary pictures? Movies so scary you couldn't go to sleep that night? When your mama said, "Good night, son," you said, "Ma, leave the light on."

I was watching *Dawn of the Dead* the other night—the one where the whole town was dead. And everybody is walking around the whole town like zombies. And these five people lock themselves up in the house. Now, first of all, some people are supposed to die. But if the whole town is dead, you don't lock yourself up in no house. Use common sense. Common sense ain't common. If I was in a town, and the whole town is dead, I wouldn't lock myself up in no house. I would walk outside and act like I was one of those sumbitches. I'd have my car keys in my got-damned hand.

When you do things, you do things for a certain reason. I been with my wife 25 years. I wouldn't trade it for the world because you learn. You can't fuck no more. And outside pussy is dangerous. Ask Clinton. Now everybody say he's a dog. Yes, he was wrong, I'm not going to condone it. But they say he was wrong because he fucked her in the White House. Where was he going to take her? Holiday Inn? What the president gon' take her to the Holiday Inn for? He shoulda fucked in the bathroom like what the fuck he did: "Here, suck it, suck it!" If you can't talk nasty to your wife or tell her, "Suck it, bitch, suck it," get somebody to suck it and say, "Suck it, you muthafucka you!" Anytime a woman save a dress with some sperm on it, that's how you talk to her: "Suck it, you filthy bitch, suck it!"

I ain't gon' lie to you, I love me some oral sex. When a woman do me, it just drives me crazy. I can't control myself. Last time I had oral sex, it was years ago. That woman was something else. I'm looking for that heifer right now. Oral sex just make you do things, say things. You ever had a woman give you oral sex and look at you? What are you looking at me for? Concentrate! Focus!

I'm just kidding. People love nasty jokes. I don't know why people like fuck jokes. I'm not telling no more fuck jokes. I'm tired of fucking. I'm tired!

It's all about love. I tell my family these are just jokes. Jokes got their place. But jokes don't tell people who you are. You got to know yourself, love yourself. I don't care nothing about y'all liking me. Because I like me my got-damned self. When I get done telling jokes, then I'm the real got-damned man. When I'm on stage, these is jokes. Jokes! When I'm on stage, it's just a half an hour of bull-shit. That's what I tell my auntie.

See, my auntie is a real superficial woman. She like material shit, she care about what people think about her. She treat all the kids real bad, except for her kid, Tyree, with his stuttering half-retarded ass. Naw, I don't mean no harm. I call it like I see it. He ain't retarded, he be playing like he retarded. Ain't nothing wrong with that sum'bitch. That sum'bitch is smart. Everytime it's time to clean up or something, he goes into his act, saying, *"Ooo-ew."* If you tell him to pick up something, he goes right into that, *"Ooo-ew!"* I say that sum'bitch faking like a sum'bitch. He read when he wants to. And when he want to play or something, his eyes straighten up and everything. But when you get on him or disci-pline him: "Ooo-ew!" And he stutter real bad. He's one of them shaky-stuttering sum'bitches.

And my auntie treat him like he's a prince. She got the school bus picking this boy up, and the school right across the street. Now when he's playing, he walks regular. Now when she tell him to walk to school or something, he start walking all like a cripple: *"Ooo-ew!"* Ain't nothing wrong with that bastard!

So, he's on the corner waiting for the school bus. Now, he stut-ter real bad. He's one of them shaky-stuttering sum'bitches. So the school bus pull up, doors open. He say, *"Ah-ah-ah-ah-ooo-ew!"* Bus driver closed the door and drove the fuck off. Next day, same cor-ner. He's standing on the corner. School bus pull up, doors open. Aw, he's mad now.

He went home and told my aunt. She's mad now: "Ah, we ain't having this shit here. I'm going to school with you in the morning. And I wish that bus driver would drive off. It's gon' be all in the news." She took her time walking him to the corner the next morn-ing. She got her video camera and everything. Bus driver pulled up, opened the door. He did it again: *"Ah-ah-ooo-ew!"* The bus driver closed the door. My auntie jumped at him: "Hold on, black bastard, hold on! What's your got-damned problem denying this boy his education?" The bus driver jumped off the bus and said, *"Ah-ah-ah-ah-ooo-ew—* He was teasing me!"

Boy, black people are something else. I been black a long time, don't tell me nothing about black people. My wife talk all the muthafucking time. Black folks talk too got-damned much. But when it come time to tell, we don't say shit. Your wife go on vacation and muthafucking neighbor say, "I saw you come in late last night. Who was that with you?" But let somebody break in your house.

> BLACK MAN (to neighbor): Did you see anything?
> NEIGHBOR: Naw, naw. I don't want to get involved. I ain't see shit.

And you can't fire a black person. You know it's going to be some shit. It ain't never a good time to fire a black person. Always going to be some controversy. If you fire him in the morning, he got a problem with it.

> BOSS: Hey Bernie, before you punch in, can you come over here? Can I talk to you?
> BLACK MAN: Yeah, what's the problem?
> BOSS: Uh, uh, we don't need you anymore.
> BLACK MAN: You let me come all the way down here to tell me this bullshit?

If you fire them at the end of the day, it's a problem.

> BOSS: Bernie, can you come into my office?
> BLACK MAN: Yeah, what's the problem?

BOSS: We don't need you no more.

BLACK MAN: You let me work all muthafucking day, and you gon' tell me this?

White person get fired, y'all go home. Y'all get understanding, Ya'll got supports. Relationships. A white guy gets fired:

BOSS: Joe, can you come into my office?

WHITE MAN: What seems to be the problem, Bob?

BOSS: I won't need you anymore.

WHITE MAN: Aw, got-damn, Bob. You're downsizing, huh?

He'll go home to his wife.

WHITE MAN: Honey, can I talk to you? Got-damnit, they let me go today. But we're going to make it. We're going to find a way to fucking make it. With your support, I can do any fucking thing.

Us? Shit, we got to walk the street for two days thinking, "What the fuck am I going to tell this bitch?" When you go home, you got to be quick:

BLACK MAN (to wife): Honey! Honey, come on in here, let me talk to you.

And they gon' turn you off as soon as they come in the room.

BLACK WIFE: What the fuck is it?

BLACK MAN: Well, sit down.

BLACK WIFE: I can't sit down! I'm cooking.

BLACK MAN: Well, baby, I want to tell you something.

Uh . . . Uh . . . Uh . . . They laid me off this afternoon.

BLACK WIFE: Laid you off? Muthafucka, you gon' have to get the fuck outta here. I can do bad all by my mutha-fucking self.

There's a big difference between a black woman and a white woman. You can shake a white woman. You can't even look like you wanna shake a sister.

BLACK WOMAN: Put your hands on me. Come on, put your muthafucking hands on me!

Kids ain't nothing but some little-ass grown-ups. Columbine, Colorado would never happen to me because I'd be looking. Kids would be like:

KID: What are you in my room for?

ME: Because I fucking can be. And let me see something I don't like. It's gon' be a misunderstanding. It's gon' be some furniture moving around this muthafucka.

Time-out is some bullshit. I don't play them fucking games. See, our generation dropped the ball with their kids. We talk about we want to give our kids more than what we had. Naw, more ain't bet-ter. See, we fucked up. Don't you hate it when your relatives bring their kids over your house and they jumping on your furniture and shit?

RELATIVE: Aw, he ain't gon' hurt nothing. Don't worry about it.

ME: Because the shit ain't yours, that's why you ain't wor-ried about it. Get that ugly bastard off my couch!

*　*　*

I'll babysit your kids all day if you let me hit them. If I babysit your kids, you won't need no hidden camera to see how I'm treating them. You come pick your kid up and he got a knot on the corner of his fucking head, don't ask what happened to your kid. I took a hammer and slapped the fuck out of him! When he got a rope burn around his neck, it's because I tried to hang the fuck out of his ass.

I'll tell you something else I don't like. I hate the fuck out of funerals. Black funerals? I ain't going to another funeral. I ain't going to my own funeral. I went to my cousin's funeral the other day. It was the most aggravating thing I've ever experienced in my life. I told my wife I ain't going to no more fucking funerals.

They lost my muthafucking cousin. We got to the funeral, and it was about to be four or five funerals because they done lost the body. They opened the casket, and my auntie say, "That ain't my muthafucking son! You better find my muthafucking son before I blow this muthafucka up! Find my baby! Find my baby!"

They rolled that muthafucka out, brought in another casket. It was him. But he had on black. And that was the wrong outfit that muthafucka had on. My auntie say, "That ain't the outfit I brought him! He don't like black! He wouldn't be caught dead in black! I bought him brown. Y'all better get some brown on my baby!" They roll him out, come back three minutes later, and she say, "Now that's my baby. How y'all change him so fast?" They say, "We just change the muthafucking head." All that hollering, I'd have changed the heads, too. He's dead!

That's why I ain't having no funeral. To hell with a funeral. If you can't treat me right while I'm alive, fuck it. I ain't gon' know you're there. I just wish I could stage my own death. Just play like I'm dead. So I can see the no-good sumbitches when they come to my funeral. I'd be laying there like I'm dead and I ain't dead. I just want to raise up on a few people and cuss they asses out. Oh, don't let a person come by that owe me some money. That's when I'm going to grab their fucking arm: "Aw, hell naw, hell naw! You got my money?" You know you want to do that. Don't you want to tell people off sometime? But you scared. You say, "Fuck off!" You'll tell your woman or man, "Fuck off!" But a person on the street? Naw, you say, "Let it go, let it go. I don't want no trouble, let it go."

I never thought I'd be like this. I used to be the hammer. Now I ain't nothing but the nail. I'm an oral sexer. Oral sex, if it ain't done right, will make a person fight. A woman will tell you in a minute. "Get up! Stop, get up, go on over there. I'll do it my muthafucking self." And you sit there, watching. If a man is getting it from his wife or somebody he like, it's different. If it's your wife, and she ain't doing it right:

> MAN: Hey, hey, hey! Your broke tooth is cutting it! It's jagged, it's jagged!
> WOMAN: Don't tell me how to suck a cock. I know what I'm doing!
> MAN: I'm just saying, you're cutting it. It's tender!

Now if a woman tells you "right there," she means, right there and don't move. And your back be hurting like a sumbitch, don't it? You be saying to yourself, "I'll be glad when this sumbitch come!" Oral sex is the same way. She saying, "Ooooh! Ooooh!" "Oooh" make me sick. "Ooooh" means you gon' be licking for four more hours.

I was over my brother's house the other day, and my nephew came in. Me and my brother are playing pool, and he says, "Daddy what's the difference between a hypothetical question and a realistic question?"

My brother, he's kinda slow, too. He says, "They basically mean the same thing, but sometimes they're different, sometimes. For example," he said, "go upstairs and ask your mother if she would make love to the mailman for $250,000."

My nephew went upstairs and came back and said, "Daddy, Mama said she'd make love to the mailman, the milk man, and any other man for $250,000."

My brother said, "Go downstairs and ask your sister if would she make love to the next door neighbor for $250,000."

He ran downstairs and came back three minutes later. He said, "Daddy, she said she would make love to the next door neighbor and the whole neighborhood in the next block for $250,000."

My brother looked at me. I looked at him. He said, "Son, sit down. See, son, hypothetically speaking, we should have half a million dollars." He said, "But realistically speaking son, we live with two hoes!"